# True Stories of the Top End

Ken White

**Books by the same author:**

*Criado: A Story of East Timor* (Indra Publishing) 2002

*Animal Rescue* (Regal Publications) 1994

# True Stories of the Top End

## Ken White

## Indra Publishing

Indra Publishing
PO Box 7, Briar Hill, Victoria, 3088, Australia.

Typeset in Palatino by Indra Publishing.
Made and Printed in Australia by Griffin Press.
Map by Tony Fankhauser Mapping Services.

National Library of Australia
Cataloguing-in-Publication data:

White, Ken, 1936- .
True stories of the Top End.

ISBN 1 920787 07 0.

1. Northern Territory - History - 20th century.  I. Title.

994.2904

# Contents

Ken White worked as a journalist for the *Northern Territory News* in Darwin for fourteen years during the 1970s and 1980s. Although he specialised in court and police reporting, he covered the civil war in East Timor and the subsequent Indonesian invasion, as well as the reconstruction of Darwin after Cyclone Tracy.

During his time in Darwin Ken was correspondent for *The Canberra Times* and *The Australian*. He began his career in metropolitan journalism with the old Sydney *Truth* in 1958 after serving a cadetship with the now Murdoch-owned Cumberland Newspapers. He then worked as a police roundsman and court reporter on the Sydney *Daily Mirror*.

*This book is dedicated to that unique breed of Australians,
the Territorians.*

Warning to Aboriginal and Torres Strait Islander readers.

Several stories in this book contain the names of deceased
Aboriginal people.

# FOREWORD

Although romantic, the notion that the Northern Territory, and Darwin in particular, is somehow not part of Australia is just another myth perpetuated and encouraged in the Australian mindset. It is an endearing concept, just as much for Territorians as for so-called Southerners. The reality is that the Territory's history, from early days to recent times, is very much Australian and has made a vast contribution to building a nation... economically and socially. That reality continues today.

It is true that Outback Australia generally has always been a more acceptable image to have in the national psyche and an easy and simplistic image to spread here and beyond our shores. Yet Australians know that when it comes to generalities, the Outback is not our model; the population, wealth, politics and power have always been, and are increasingly, urban based. It seems to matter little that a large chunk of that wealth, politics and power, traces back to the bush... then and now.

It is a numbers game. Several large suburbs in Sydney and Melbourne have populations as big as the Northern Territory's and certainly bigger than Darwin's.

It is this extraordinary imbalance in population, added to politics and power that has prevented the Northern Territory from becoming a state. In the mid-1970s, the then Queensland Premier, Joh Bjelke-Petersen, through the High Court, stopped statehood because he (and no doubt many other federal and state politicians) did not want to contend with another Tasmanian situation; in effect, a large number of senators being elected by a small number of voters and controlling national politics. Instead, the Northern Territory was given self-government (and provides a harmless enough Senate representation of two, which in the numbers game means one from each of the two main parties).

This official attitude of 'you are not quite grown-up yet' permeates thinking and attitudes about the Territory from the vast majority of Australians, not least the decision-makers of the southern-controlled media. Even after a quarter of a century of self-government, plus the advent of fast and accessible broadcasting communications, the media, with some exceptions, still have difficulty in applying the same values of news importance to the Northern Territory as they do to the states. Unless, of course, it is a disaster or a so-called 'Aboriginal problem', which the mass media usually gets embarrassingly wrong because it is not equipped to focus on a complex situation – it sees Aboriginal affairs coverage as getting film and a few quotes about a gang fight in Redfern.

But let's not get too serious. There should be more light-hearted, funny stories in our media. Like the Sydney *Sun-Herald* headline 'Better Than Baygon', recording the reason a man in a Darwin Court gave for waking up the neighbourhood by shooting holes through his tin roof with a rifle: he was aiming at cockroaches. Yes, perhaps that could only happen in Darwin, and there are many other 'Believe It Or Not' stories from there.

But those stories and even more high-profile events, such as a dingo running off with a baby, were characterised as being extraordinary, possibly because they took place in the NT. And with the Azaria Chamberlain case there were religious and Aboriginal cameo parts played out to the media's delight. The Northern Territory is not a mystical never-never land. And if there do appear to be Peter Pans and Wendys, or others who either never want to grow up, or are just plain eccentric, then that's great for the human race. But any town or suburb, anywhere in Australia, has probably got their fair share.

The Northern Territory is very part of Australia's yesteryear and present everyday. Its importance, based on such few people, is what is extraordinary – the early exploration, telegraph communications, aviation, rural development, Wave Hill and the Aboriginal justice and land rights movement to name a few. And then there are court trials such as the Chamberlain case that have not only challenged Australia's vaunted justice system and found it wanting, but also failed the national public test of giving everyone a fair go.

At the time of the Chamberlain case, the public show of blind and ignorant prejudice in Darwin itself, which spread nationwide along with inane and cruel jokes, was a blight on the Territory's history, albeit a passing one. But it has not diminished the extraordinary good that Territorians have given the national image, because these images have not come from urban or rural myths but from reality... the mateship among men and women, sharing and giving a willing hand of survival when nature and human enemy throws everything at you, being who you are and doing your best and knowing that's all that's expected of you. And Darwin has taken that part of Aussie doctrine one step further and given the rest of Australia a social challenge that it has yet to fully and wholeheartedly take up: harmony among groups who are diverse in their nationalities, religions and cultures. Perfection in this has not yet been achieved, particularly in regard to Australia's own Aboriginals, but the situation is vastly better than the uninformed might believe. And it must be remembered that Darwin has always had to be many years ahead of the rest of Australia in accepting New Australians... Chinese, Vietnamese and Timorese, to name a few. The fact that Darwin may be nearer to Asia than it is to any other big Australian city is said to have something to do with it. I doubt it. Darwin is Australia and proud of it. In return, Australians should be proud of Darwin and show it a bit more respect, take it a bit more seriously. I did not do so until some years after I had spent four years in Darwin following the 1974 cyclone. I was single and young, and my answer to a friend who asked why I was going to Sydney, was 'It's time to return to the real world'. He replied: 'You're leaving it'. It was one of those typically penetrating, disarming Territorian statements that proclaim a self-evident fact. I have never adequately been able to challenge it.

The stories of the Northern Territory in this book are many and varied, mostly important and always eye-opening and entertaining. I'm sure that if you have never been to the top end of Australia, they will help you to see it in a new light. Then go!

Ted Cowham, ex Northern Territory
journalist and editor, Melbourne

# AUTHOR'S NOTE & ACKNOWLEDGEMENTS

This is a series of true stories (and a few journalistic reminiscences) set in the Northern Territory, most of which happened in the 1970s and 80s. I have, however, attempted to give a glimpse of what Darwin was like in its earlier years and some of the dramatic events that helped to make it the unique place it is today. I have also included the story of the Aboriginal folk hero, Nemarluk, one of the great sagas of the Territory, and the highly controversial judgements handed down by Mr Justice Tommy Wells, who advocated flogging as a punishment for Aborigines. In one or two cases the better-known former names of Aboriginal settlements have been used and only in one story – the homicide at the Adelaide River War Cemetery – have the names been changed.

I am very much indebted to former Darwin solicitor, Neil Halfpenny, for his invaluable assistance and in fostering my interest in Nemarluk. I would like to thank Darwin barrister, Ray Minahan, for giving me access to the unpublished files pertaining to the Michael and Lindy Chamberlain case and also Solicitor General and former magistrate, Tom Pauling, for permission to use parts of his Seminar on Aboriginal Customary Law. For certain details of the careers of Territory judges, I have referred to Judge Dean Mildren's and Peter Elder's short biographies published in the *Northern Territory Dictionary of Biography*, Vols. 2 and 3 (Northern Territory University Press 1992 and 1996). Among others who have helped in one way or another are Richard Creswick, Communications Advisor, Office of the Chief Minister, former colleague and journalist, Kerry Sharpe, the staff at both the Melbourne and Adelaide State Libraries and, last but not least, Annette Harrison, of the Wyndham City Library.

Ken White, Melbourne

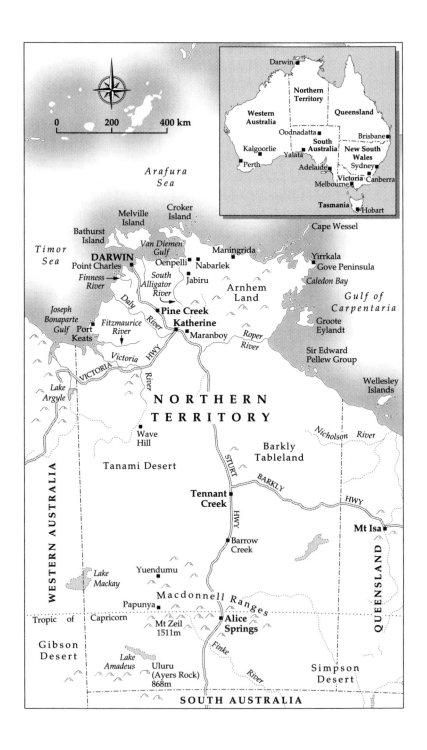

# INTRODUCTION

Much to the discomfiture of the Crown in the Northern Territory, there was a marked reluctance on the part of juries to convict. During the latter part of the nineteenth century the Crown, in fact, shared the problems of their counterpart in Queensland when, for example, one Harry Redford was acquitted in the Roma Court of cattle stealing, despite the fact that he confessed to taking one thousand head of them and selling them in Adelaide. In 1892, Mr Justice Dashwood, after presiding over a murder trial in Darwin, penned a report to the Governor in which he pointed out that at the close of a very strong Crown case, the foreman of the jury immediately jumped to his feet and stated that the jury was not satisfied with the evidence and returned a verdict of not guilty. In the course of his report, His Honour said: 'Had the duty developed upon me of deciding as to the guilt or innocence of the prisoners, I should have had no alternative but to find them guilty of deliberate and wilful murder. Fortunately for them, the responsibility of finding the verdict rested with the jury.' A report of the case was later published in a newspaper called the Public Service Review. Under the heading 'An Astonished Judge' the author wrote:

> Imagine the intense surprise in the court, especially on the Bench, when the foreman announced the verdict, and the look of profound astonishment that came over the judge's face was something to remember. His Honour looked at the jury and the jury looked at the judge. Nothing was said, but the glances which the judge and jury exchanged conveyed probably more than words could express in the marked silence of the courthouse. Finally, His

Honour rose, collected his papers, turned to the jury, solemnly surveyed them with those expressive eyes of his and, after a prolonged pause, simply but significantly said, 'Good-day gentlemen,' and left the Bench.

In cases involving Aborigines, juries, more often than not, brought in a not guilty verdict. In fact, so reluctant were juries, particularly in Alice Springs, to convict Aborigines of crimes committed on other Aborigines that one judge, the late Mr Justice Kriewaldt, in exasperation, 'came to the conclusion that the system of trial by jury should be abolished where the accused was an Aborigine' There was no doubt in his mind, he said, that many jurors had given effect to the view that Aborigines should never be tried in white courts by returning verdicts of not guilty where the evidence had established guilt. There had been cases in Alice Springs 'where the verdict, in my opinion, can be explained on no other basis.' Nor did the judge have much faith in Darwin juries where, until civil servants became eligible for jury service, the same outlook existed. Very few members of a Darwin jury had been able to understand the 'pidgin' counsel used to examine an Aboriginal witness, and still fewer were able to understand the real import of the scanty answers given by the witness. The judge cited two notorious Darwin cases in which the jury dug their toes in and refused to convict, even though the evidence was sufficient to have entitled them to hand down a verdict of either murder or manslaughter. Each case involved part Aboriginal people, Maroney and Lucy O'Donnell. Both were charged with the murder of white persons and both were acquitted. He therefore had adopted the view 'that the average person called on for jury duty, where the accused was an Aborigine, was faced with a task that was beyond his powers.' However, it was also true that juries stubbornly refused to convict whites accused of crimes against Aborigines. Available files revealed that cases where white men were tried for the murder of an Aborigine all resulted in acquittals.

His Honour's observations were made about the middle of last century, but the problem of recalcitrant juries lasted into the 1980s. In November, 1981, cock-a-hoop Crown prosecutors quaffed quite a number of celebratory beers to mark the first verdict of murder brought in by a Darwin jury in eight years and the second in thirteen. With the rate of homicides per head of population in the Territory four times the national average, it was high time, many prosecutors felt, to scrap the time-honoured jury system and substitute a panel of judges. One celebrated case where the Crown went all out for a murder conviction and refused a 'sweetheart' plea to manslaughter involved a Finn who, after a squabble, shot a fellow countryman three times while he was watching TV. Failing to kill the man, the accused casually walked up to him as he lay on the ground, held his .22 calibre rife at his head and administered the coup de grace. To the disgust of the Crown, the jury opted for manslaughter. In another trial that caused considerable interest, a well-known Darwin woman was charged with attempted murder after shooting her husband. The jury settled for the far lesser count of unlawful wounding. The trial judge, Sir William Forster, whose summing up was decidedly in favour of the Crown, remarked privately after the case that juries 'can sometimes come up with the most extraordinary decisions.'

If juries showed traits of eccentricity and perhaps perverseness so, too, did some of the characters that dispensed justice. There was Justice Tommy Wells, an ex-boxer endowed with multiple idiosyncrasies and who, after a female witness complained about the way she was being cross-examined, refused the interrogating solicitor permission to proceed and denied him the right to appear in the court. There was Mr Justice David Bevan, a supporter of the abolition of trial by jury, who had the rare distinction of being told that the public could not and did not regard him as a judge, that his protégé the stipendiary magistrate was 'a caterpillar and sycophant of a corrupt Administration' and that it was felt there were no courts of justice for citizens in Darwin. He was, it was stated in a series of resolutions passed by the Town Council, the all-round legal hand of the government. 'You have sat too long here for any good you have been doing. Depart and let us have done with you. In the name of God, go.' A year later, in September 1920, a small notice in the *Commonwealth Gazette* announced that Judge Bevan had been removed from office. Ironically, as a result of an appeal to the High Court for wrongful dismissal, he received a not inconsiderable settlement (for those days) for two thousand, eight hundred pounds. Then there was London-born Ross Ibbotson Dalton Mallam 'a Conrad-like character, (according to his friend, the Australian poet Frederick Macartney) 'with his tropical suit, his topee and a beard [that came] down to his waist,' who, as a flamboyant barrister in Darwin prior to his appointment as a judge, helped found the Goose Club, a small group of men including the editor of the *Northern Territory Times*, Fred Thompson, and a police sergeant who would meet on the corner of Mitchell Street and The Esplanade every evening to discuss public affairs, criticise the Administration and advocate the abolition of the public service. While still practising as a barrister, he had a monumental row with special magistrate and deputy Supreme Court judge, Major Gerald Hogan, who struck Mallam off the register over an alleged misfeasance. Not one to avoid a stoush, Mallam hurried south and appealed to the High Court that found in his favour and nullified his suspension. As a concession to his elevation to the Bench, Mallam trimmed his waist-length beard to a short goatee. He died in 1954 (the same year as Bevan and Wells) most likely of malnutrition, not a common cause of death among judges. His predecessor, Donald Arthur Roberts, described as 'a full bodied man with a deliberate manner offset by a quiet sense of humour,' was hardly a role model for How to Win Friends and Influence People. He made it quite clear that he disliked or 'loathed' most of the personnel in the public service and went so far as to have the Territory's first Crown Law officer, Algernon Charles Braham, evicted from his accommodation in the courthouse. He also managed to get rid of stipendiary magistrate and deputy Supreme Court judge, Gerald Hogan, who he had transferred to New Guinea. After failing to gain the post of Administrator that he sought in addition to his position as judge, he moved to Mt Gambier in South Australia where he set up his own legal practice.

Many Territory judges, however, showed remarkable restraint and tolerance. Mr Justice Muirhead, for example, pointedly ignored a heated outburst from a Sydney journalist who, as the jury filed out after convicting Michael and Lindy Chamberlain in the famous Azaria case, yelled out 'You pack of mongrel bastards.'

Much as been said and written about the Territory, but perhaps nothing more apt than the words spoken by the Chief justice, Sir William Forster, on the occasion of his farewell in 1985: 'I will have – I will take with me, many fond memories... which, in themselves, are not perhaps terribly important, but they do tend to be indicative of what you might describe, perhaps, as the ethos of the Territory. It's no good pretending and it's no good being arrogant about it either, but the Territory's a somewhat different place to other places, and this has been one of its charms as far as I've been concerned.'

# THE EARLY YEARS

'A God-forsaken hole' – Viscount Kenmure, 1880

'The more I saw of this place the more intriguing it became. The South was a colourless mass of nonentities. Here people were individuals, with a sense of hospitality that equalled that of the Arab nomad' – Captain C.T.G. Haultain, 1936.

There was a time when it didn't have a particularly good reputation. String together a list of derogative adjectives used to describe Darwin in its early years and it would read like an entry in Roget's under the word 'dirty.' It was a place where the smells were strong enough to knock anyone down. The sea breeze was 'like the pestilential smell from a boiling down factory.' People lived in accommodation no better than Aboriginal wurlies while the local medico, Dr Samuel Ellison, 'wanders about from day to day seeking a place to lay his head and hang his mosquito net.' If a public servant vacated anything in the shape of a hut, three or four others 'make a dash for it; they are like hermit crabs waiting for each other's shells'.

No one, in fact, had anything good to say about the place. A notably disenchanted visitor was the British nobleman, Viscount Kenmure, who sailed into the port in 1880, looked around and thought glumly of England. He was not surprised, he said, that the people down south characterised Darwin as a God-forsaken hole with only a sheet of brown paper between it and Hades. Apart from the stench and squalor, the roads turned into muddy tracks during the wet season and ribbons of dust during the dry. The local paper lamented at one stage that the 'horrible conditions' that prevailed at the cemetery during heavy rains were one of the strongest arguments in favour of a system of cremation. 'The exigencies of a tropical climate make it imperative that a number of graves be kept prepared to meet possible emergencies, and during heavy rains these become filled with water and frequently this water becomes impregnated with nameless and nauseous impurities. To this was added, at a recent funeral, constant thunder and lightning, accompanied by driving wind and rain. The coffin was lowered into the water-filled grave, but would not sink. The undertaker and only mourner had to get down into the grave and stand on the lid until sufficient earth had been shovelled to prevent the coffin rising to the surface.'

Darwin was, admittedly, a place like none other in Australia. In its brief and extraordinary history since white settlement it experienced destructive cyclones – six in the period from 1878 to 1974 – a rebellion that overthrew the government authority, forty-six Japanese bombing raids and perhaps the greatest calamity of all, the loss in 1875 of about a quarter of its population in a shipping disaster.

In 1863, the year after explorer John McDouall Stuart's epic journey from south to north through the Centre, South Australia wrested control of the Northern Territory from New South Wales, letters Patent being transferred with the Territory in July that year. It was a move the young colony was to regret. By an unfortunate piece of muddled thinking, Lieutenant-Colonel Boyle Travers Finness, a former British army officer better known by his opponents as BTF or Bloody Tom Fool who was appointed the first Government Resident of the Territory, chose Escape Cliffs at the mouth of the Adelaide River for a settlement, convinced that the flood plains would be an ideal area for agricultural success.

The 'startling circumstances' from which Escape Cliffs received its name is described in a humorous entry in the diary of Captain J Lort Stokes.

A few days after my interview in the dinghy with the natives', Captain Stokes wrote, 'Mr Fitzmaurice went ashore to compare the compasses. From the quantity of iron contained in the rocks it was necessary to select a spot free from their influence. A sandy beach at the foot of [the] cliffs was accordingly chosen. The observations had been commenced, and were almost half completed, when, on the summit of the cliffs, which arose about twenty feet above our heads, suddenly appeared a large party of natives with poised and quivering spears, as if about immediately to deliver them. Stamping on the ground and shaking their heads to and fro they threw out their long shaggy locks in a circle, whilst their glaring eyes flashed with fury, as they champed and spat out the ends of their long beards, a custom with Australian natives when in a state of violent excitement. They were evidently in earnest and bent on mischief. It was therefore not a little surprising to behold their paroxysm of rage evaporated before the happy presence of mind displayed by Mr Fitzmaurice, in immediately beginning to dance and shout though in momentary expectation of being pierced by a dozen spears. In this he was imitated by Mr Keys who was assisting in the operations, and who at the moment was a little distance off and might have escaped. Without, however thinking of himself, he very nobly joined his companion in amusing the natives; and they succeeded in diverting themselves from their evident evil designs, until a boat landing in a bay nearby drew their attention. The foremost of this party was recognised to be the ill-looking fellow who [had] left me in the canoe with a revengeful scowl upon his face. Messrs Fitzmaurice and Keys had firearms lying on the ground within reach of their hands; the instant however they ceased dancing and attempted to touch them a dozen spears were pointed at their breasts. Their lives hung upon a threat and their escape must be regarded as truly wonderful, and only to be attributed to the happy readiness with which they adapted themselves to the perils of the situation. This was the last we saw of the natives in Adam Bay, and the meeting is likely to be long remembered by some and not without pleasant reflections; for although, at the time it was just looked upon as a very serious affair, it was afterwards proved to be a great source of mirth. No one could recall to mind, without laughing, the ludicrous figures necessarily cut by our shipmates when to amuse the natives they figured on the light fantastic toe.

And so Escape Cliffs was named.

Under Finness' less than inspired direction, the settlement was a spectacular failure. As a seaport and city, the place was 'worthless' while a 'greater sense of waste and desolation could not be imagined.'

One of Finness' first actions, unsurprisingly given the man's character, was to 'teach the blacks a lesson.' After a number of thefts he authorised a 'punitive party' of sixteen men, seven of them mounted, to shoot Aborigines on sight. With Finness' son, Frederick, leading the expedition, an unknown number of Aborigines were shot at random. It was, wrote Territory historian, Peter Forrest, 'the end of the Larrakeyah dreaming'. Recalled to Adelaide to appear before a Royal Commission to account for the debacle, BTF was censured for mismanagement, tactlessness and waste of time, labour and money. From his photograph one sees a man with a large round face, graced with mutton-chop whiskers. The severe line of compressed lips hints at obstinacy and arrogance while the basilisk-like eyes stare stonily beneath bushy brows and thinning hair.

When it became obvious that Escape Cliffs was doomed as a viable settlement, the Surveyor-General of South Australia, George Woodroffe Goyder, or Little Energy as his men called him, who became the first Government Resident at Palmerston (re-named Darwin in 1911), set out from Adelaide with more than a hundred men on the barque *Moonta*, sailed into Port Darwin and established a settlement.

Goyder was succeeded by twelve government residents – at one stage there was an unworkable situation when there was one for North Australia and another for Central Australia – until 1911 when the Territory was handed over by South Australia to Canberra.

By the turn of the century, however, it had become obvious to South Australia that running the Territory was costing far too much, estimated at about one hundred and thirty thousand pounds annually. Resurrecting the city after the devastating cyclone of 1897 – 'a gentle reminder from Providence', one preacher mildly observed, 'that we are a very sinful people' – was an added burden. A few options were mooted – give it back to England (obviously untenable and the British Colonial Office showed no interest anyway), put the whole lot up for private sale (there wasn't even an offer) or transfer control to the new Commonwealth. Ironically, South Australia pushed for a condition to be attached to the transfer – an early completion of an Adelaide-Darwin rail link!

The government residents and administrators were a disparate lot. Among the earlier ones there was the unpopular Bloomfield Douglas (1870-73) a former clipper captain, who was officially rebuked for inefficiency. His successor, George Byng Scott, was paranoid about the 'great number of government employers who were given to drink.' Then there was the unconventional, intolerant and tactless Dr John Anderson Gilruth, (1912-1919) the first administrator under Commonwealth control and a veritable William Bligh of the Territory. Dubbed 'The Lord High Overall' and described by the Melbourne *Herald* as 'a tall, gaunt, iron-grey Scotchman, [with a] deep bass voice, a stern expression of countenance and in manner abrupt,' he eventually found himself deadlocked in a power struggle with unionists. The issue had been simmering for five years, amid a series of scandals and allegations of corruption and collusion, and resulted in the first overthrow of government authority since the Rum Rebellion in 1808. On December 18, 1918, a crowd of men, numbering between seven hundred and a thousand and headed by an effigy of Gilruth, marched on Government House. Fearing civil disorder and obviously alarmed, Gilruth and Judge Bevan who, in addition to his duties as the only Supreme Court judge, was a business associate of the administrator, armed about thirty civil servants with rifles, revolvers and loaded sticks. The men had passed a resolution asking Gilruth to address them on their grievances or, failing that, 'he be asked if he is willing to leave the Territory by steamer and remain away until such times as a public commission is granted on his administration.' Bevan was also asked to 'comply regarding his judiciary administration to the same extent' as Gilruth.

Initially, Gilruth refused to address the men, a deputation being met at his office by a special constable armed with a loaded stick, an action labelled by the mayor, Cr Douglas Watts, as 'a display of despotism.' Impatient, the men demanded that 'within five minutes' Gilruth should appear before them and 'vindicate his attitude.' Again, Gilruth refused, saying he was answerable only to the Minister and, in the circumstances, would not and did not recognise the citizens. The men then gave Gilruth one minute and the Administrator capitulated. Under the headline 'Armed Disturbance at Darwin,' the Melbourne

*Herald's* correspondent reported the scene: 'On his appearance, the chairman requested him to address the meeting from the platform. He spoke, however, from inside Government House grounds. His position was much lower than the ground on which the citizens were standing. They pressed forward to hear his remarks and their weight caused the fence to collapse. A free fight ensued, in which the police, special constables and populace participated. During the melee which followed firearms were discharged and bludgeons were used. The populace, it is asserted, were without arms, but they quickly disarmed the police and others who supported the administrator. Dr Gilruth, who had received a rough handling, was... enabled to escape.' The only cool head among the crowd appeared to be the Mayor, Cr Watts, who persuaded the 'rebels' to 'cease hostilities.' The crowd then burned Gilruth's effigy, throwing captured rifles into the flames. Two months later, Gilruth and his family were evacuated on the Australian warship, *HMAS Encounter*. Judge Bevan and two senior officials followed soon afterwards. Like the Rum Rebellion a hundred and ten years previously, none of the ringleaders was seriously punished. Their leader, Harold Nelson, went on to become the Territory's first member of the House of Representatives, a position he held from 1922 to 1934. Thirty-nine years later his son Jock was appointed Administrator.

The disgraced Gilruth later returned to England on full pay and died, aged sixty-six, in 1934. The 'partisan' Judge Bevan, Gilruth's 'intimate friend and daily companion' who 'the public could not and do not regard as a judge,' according to the terms of a motion carried by the Town Council, became an orchardist in Upper Beaconsfield in Victoria and died in 1954.

For the next fifty-nine years the Territory was run by a succession of Federal Government Departments, although an elected Legislative Council, set up in 1947 with an original membership of seven government members and six elected members, had limited autonomy. As a sop, the Territory was granted representation by one member with limited powers in the Federal Parliament. Finally, on July 1, 1978, Canberra handed over most (but not all) powers to the Country-liberal Party-dominated Government headed by a young solicitor, Paul Everingham.

The initial move to set up a judiciary in Darwin ended in a calamity. Proposals in the early 1870s in the South Australian parliament for a separate Northern Territory Supreme Court were defeated and instead the South Australian Governor proclaimed a new circuit district for the Supreme Court of South Australia. This was to be known as the Palmerston circuit district (Darwin originally was called Palmerston after Britain's prime minister) and encompassed the whole of the Northern Territory. Sittings, presided over by the then third South Australian judge, Mr Justice Wearing, were to begin on February 8, 1875. The judge was offered a bonus to make the dangerous journey by ship from Adelaide to Palmerston, but declined this emolument, requesting only that the government pay the additional premiums on his insurance policy. This was tragically prescient because His Honour and all his staff, returning to Adelaide, were drowned when the *S.S. Gothenburg*, less than a week after leaving Darwin, struck a reef near Bowen off the Queensland coast during a cyclone and foundered. It was one of Australia's greatest maritime disasters. One hundred and two passengers – about a quarter of Darwin's white population who were on their first furlough since coming to the Territory – perished. Only twenty-two men survived the sinking. Among those drowned were Minnie Price, wife of the Government Resident and magistrate, Edward Price, and their five children, several girls on their way to school in Adelaide, and the wife and three children from an earlier marriage, of the retiring colonial surgeon Dr Millner.

From then on South Australia was not prepared to hazard any more of her Supreme Court judges. As a result, the Northern Territory Justice Act of 1875 was passed, allowing for commissions to be issued on an ad hoc basis to lawyers and special magistrates. They were empowered to deal with all manner of civil and criminal matters, except those which carried the death penalty which still had to be dealt with in Adelaide. In those early days commissions were usually issued about every six months to the Government Resident, who almost invariably was also appointed a special magistrate. Not all were lawyers. Those charged with breaking the law in the early 1890s were brought before an architect, John George Knight. Notoriously fat, Knight was, fortunately for the 'riff raff' that appeared before him, a man respected for his fairness. From an ad hoc magistrate and assistant to the Government resident, George Scott, Knight rose to become the resident and distinguished himself well.

The 1875 Justice Act was supposed to be a temporary measure; it had a two-year sunset clause. But as events turned out, it provided the framework for the administration of justice in the Territory until the Commonwealth took over some thirty-six years later when Mr Justice Samuel James Mitchell, who was also the Government Resident, became the first judge of the Supreme Court of the Northern Territory.

The two main preoccupations of the law in the early years were Aborigines and the Chinese, whose predilection for opium focussed police attention to an obsessive degree. Finness' random shooting of Aborigines at Escape Cliffs was a grisly prelude to a sporadic series of killings and reprisals that continued well into the twentieth century and that invariably involved the deaths, if not by the Martini Henry rifle, then by poisoned water holes, of blameless men, women and children. Miners and pastoralists, a South Australian Royal Commission was told in 1898, were 'shooting Aborigines like crows.' Items like the following piece of doggerel that reflected much white sentiment in the Top End appeared in the *Northern Territory Times*:

> *These white men with their loaded guns*
> *Make black men scarce as married nuns.*

Wrote Syd Kyle-Little, perhaps the Territory's most famous patrol officer, in his admirable book, *Whispering Wind – Adventures in Arnhem Land*: 'Until as late as 1890, the Colonial Government continued to ignore the official existence of the Aborigines. They were, in effect, so many buffaloes grazing the land. And as settlers and prospectors moved deeper into the heart of the country many clashes occurred and the better-armed whites, without fear of Police or Government restraint, raped and shot as the occasion demanded. As late as 1917, Aborigines in Darwin were treated little better than dogs.'

When four workers at a copper mine at the Daly River were killed by Aborigines in 1884, the same newspaper, invoking canines as a comparison, editorialised: 'They suffered the most horrible of deaths at the hand of a race of creatures resembling men in form, but with no more trace of human feelings in their natures than the Siberian wolves.' 'The right class of men,' the editorial continued, 'are now on [their] tracks... but we do not expect to hear many particulars of their chase; the less the better, in such cases as the present, it is far more sensible to avoid complications by the exercise of a judicious reticence.' Down south, the Sydney *Sun* told its readers that the 'murderous blacks must be taught a severe lesson.'

Later, when the Kahlin Compound, 'an institution for the betterment of waifs and strays among Aborigines' opened in Darwin in 1913, the local paper bemoaned that babies of all colours on the breast of Aboriginal women were a public scandal. 'Unless we wish the Territory to go to hell altogether,' it continued, 'the Government should step in and impose a heavy penalty on any white man offending in this regard. If a man is too lazy, too drunken, or too mean to get a wife of his own, then he should not be allowed to create a breed which is a menace to society.'

Aborigines didn't fare better in the Press in Alice Springs. In the late 1920s violence broke out in the pastoral country northwest of the town when a severe drought forced desert living natives to move eastwards in search of food. Wrote a reporter on the local paper, '... attacks on Nugget Morton, of Broadmeadows Station and Harry Tilmouth, of Napperby, show the niggers in this region are altogether too cheeky.' The situation rapidly deteriorated, eventually leading to the infamous Coniston killings in which more than thirty Aborigines (the exact number is not known) were shot by a party led by Mounted Constable George Murray who, a Board of Inquiry later found, had not been guilty of improper conduct

Chinese, too, suffered under the twin idols of discrimination and prejudice. During the 1880s, they regularly appeared before the court on charges relating to opium that previously had been legal and duty free. However, as a result of legislation introduced in the South Australian Parliament it was proscribed as a prohibited drug. The Chinese, who at the time numbered two thousand, seven hundred out of a total male population of three thousand, three hundred and forty-seven, excluding the children of mixed Aboriginal descent, promptly resorted to smuggling, much of which was successful. Stumbling across a box containing forty tins of raw opium that had fallen overboard from a ship and washed ashore on Melville Island, the Aborigines, unaware of what it was, found a new use for the drug – they caulked their canoes with it.

It was during this period that it seemed as if the white man's boastful declaration that they would 'triumph over nature, the Chinese and the Aborigines' would come true. Despite the important part played by Chinese immigrants in the development of the Top End (Chinese labour was used in mines as well as for essential public works, including the building of the Palmerston-Pine Creek railway) fear of the 'Yellow Peril' spread not only in the Territory, but also throughout the entire country. In Adelaide the Minister for Education, Dr John Cockburn, denounced the Chinese as 'birds of plunder who dug their gold and flew away to their homes and ended their days amidst the fumes of opium.' Inflammatory and misleading statements were bandied about, like the one published in a leading Queensland newspaper in 1882: 'Nearly all the white men who went to the Territory have either been ruined, driven out, or reduced to poverty [by the Chinese]. We believe that they have strangled nearly all European attempts at colonisation, miners and traders alike.' Admittedly, these claims were described as 'a gross libel' by William Sowden in his official narrative on the Territory entitled 'The Northern Territory As It Is' for the then South Australian Minister for the Northern Territory, J Langdon Parsons. But as recently as 1953, the Deputy Leader of the Federal Opposition, Arthur Calwell, wrongly accused Darwin Chinese of 'trafficking in teenage brides from Hong Kong.'

Restrictions were placed on Chinese immigration as early as 1888 and thirteen years later, white paranoia about the 'peril' led to the passing of the Immigration Restriction Act. In one of the most poignant episodes in Australian history, Chinese who had not paid their naturalisation fee of ten shillings began to be sent home. It was, wrote Douglas Lockwood in *The Front Door*, nemesis for the Chinese. 'Entire townships were vacant. Cyanide vats were handy for those who could not face an enforced journey and the swollen remains of one hundred men who poisoned themselves dotted the fields.' Lockwood recorded that Samuel Palmerston Brown, then a junior engineer on ships trading between Port Darwin and China, told him, 'We were sometimes little more than a floating hearse. We had dead bodies everywhere. To make it worse, the trip was often too rough for old and fatigued people. Many died on the way. Their bodies were disembowelled and stuffed with oakum. It was terrible... terrible... but it had to be done. We had contracted to deliver these people, dead or alive, to their homeland. They couldn't be buried at sea.'

Discrimination against the Chinese lasted well into the twentieth century. Charles See-Kee's experience was indicative of the general attitude.

> I was one of the first Chinese to be accepted in the Public Service as a clerical officer in the Northern Territory Administration. In those days (the early 1930s) we did have Chinese working for the Government but they were employed as houseboys, cooks or gardeners. However, although I was accepted, there were still some prejudices lingering among some of the high-brows in the public service. This soon became apparent when I was curtly informed by the Government Secretary (the top executive officer in the Northern Territory Administration at the time) that 'your application for admission to the wardroom mess has not been recommended by the committee of the civil wing of the Mess' (the Government Hostel for single public servants). Later on, when the war started and everybody was transferred to Alice Springs, I became the Secretary of the Public Service Mess in Alice Springs. Before the transfer of the Government offices to Alice Springs, the Secretary of the Public Service Mess (Government Hostel) in Darwin had gone to Canberra. He later came to Alice Springs and he had

to apply to me for admission to the Alice Springs Government Hostels. I though this was a great opportunity to get my own back and not accept his application – but I didn't.

Nevertheless, by the mid-1930s it appeared that Darwin was beginning to emerge from its dark age. According to an enthusiastic report by the Melbourne *Herald's* special correspondent, Australia's most northern city could no longer be dubbed Darwin the Damned, a name it had languished under for the previous two generations. In what was perhaps the most eulogistic pierce of writing on Darwin since its foundation in 1869, the writer said the city, for so long regarded as Australia's back door, was on its way to becoming its front door. Warming to his theme, the writer in rather hyperbolic prose continued:

> Darwin is returning, as it were, to the world picture. Distance is indeed the crux of the north and now distance, that fearful ogre of the past, is being eaten up and destroyed by modern methods of transport and the tropical north is being brought closer to Sydney and Melbourne. Here (in Darwin) is to be created the directional radio station in conjunction with that at Timor, providing a wireless direction finding beam for aircraft crossing the Timor Sea. Thus, this formerly deserted tropic sea will soon be navigated by means of the latest invention of Science; and the argosies (sic) of the air, roaring down from the north-west, will sweep across this last lap of water, 500 miles in extent, dead on their course, guided by the radio beam to Darwin straight ahead. It is one of the little realised romances of Australia.

The port and principal entrepot of the north, Australia's baby Singapore, the writer said, was being rudely wakened from its slumbers – thanks to the defence activities and to the forthcoming opening of the London Air Mail route. 'And today Darwin's future looks brighter and more promising than ever before… the scene of a new and refreshing activity.' Nevertheless there were, he admitted, a few 'special disabilities,' including its wharf, with which the city was still struggling. 'Two ships cannot berth alongside at the same time. The wharf dries, too, at low water springs, with the result that the ship alongside sits on the mud. The port's approaches are unsurveyed, though this work is now being carried out.' Concluded the correspondent: 'Aviation is its Fairy Godmother, as it is that of all the Northern Territory. Those great outback spaces with their isolated towns will soon became part and parcel of the Great Eastern Empire Truck Line – the new great Air Way that will stretch from London to New Zealand, and their isolation and remoteness will vanish like the mists of Mourne.

A year later, C T G Haultain, skipper of the *Larrakia*, the first patrol boat to police Territory waters, was to observe:

> The population of Darwin, if judged by the opinions of some of its citizens, held the unenviable reputation for the highest pro rata illegitimacy rate in the world. Have a drink at the 'Vic' and Dick, your newly found drinking companion, would assure you that Harry and Tom were 'a prime pair of bastards.' Shift your stand to the 'Don' and Harry would tell you in the strictest confidence that Tom and Dick were 'grade A1 bastards you can trust no farther than you can chuck the Roman Catholic Church.' Meet Tom, more catholic in his discriminatory powers, he spread bastardy to the

Bills, Joes, Georges, Blues and Nats, retaining special emphasis for Dick and Harry. From what I could gather, everybody knew everybody else's business, and minded it. Those not in the Government service, though having their individual likes and dislikes for people in their own coteries, were unanimous on one point. The Government servants were ALL bastards, to the newest joined recruit.

Captain Haultain went on: 'Another notable feature of Darwin was its wealth of self-appointed 'experts' on every conceivable subject, esoteric and mundane. The town had more 'authorities' than a blackfellow's dog had fleas. Ask one for his views on the 'quantum theory' and you would be lucky if you were not trampled to death in the rush of informants.'

Few Federal politicians deigned to visit Darwin in the 1930s. One who did was the Minister for Commerce and unofficial deputy Prime Minister, Sir Earle Christmas Grafton Page, but the reception he received was not one that he expected. Arrangements were made for him to be brought from the Qantas flying boat by dinghy to the patrol boat *Larrakia* and then ferried to the wharf where a welcoming committee, including the Administrator, C L Abbott, would be waiting. The aircraft landed, and the dinghy made fast alongside the passenger exit. Sir Earle appeared and the coxswain, Bill Myles, extended a hand to help him into the boat. Instead, Sir Earle turned his back and lowered one foot that Myles tried to guide to the bottom of the boat. Ignoring the proffered help by kicking the hand away, the MP put his other foot onto the gunwale with the result that the boat capsized, throwing both Myles and Sir Earle into the sea. Myles managed to right the dinghy, at the same time holding the spluttering Sir Earle by the scruff of the neck whom he eventually managed to heave back on board. Sir Earle was far from amused, letting loose a stream of invective at the coxswain. Myles, however, didn't take the abuse lying down and was overheard loudly telling Sir Earle he was 'a silly old goat' and instructed the fuming politician to 'sit still in the flaming boat, or you'd have us in the bloody drink again.' Finally, a red-faced and bedraggled MP staggered ashore to be greeted by a horrified and embarrassed reception committee. Sir Earle's well known 'distinctive and frequent laugh that enabled him to chortle his way out of many an embarrassing corner' was noticeably absent on this occasion. It was the last visit of a Federal politician until after the end of the war.

For some time now there has been a perceived romance associated with the Territory. But violence has never been far from the surface. Writing in 1991, shortly before his death, Alice Springs magistrate, Denis Barritt, made this observation: 'We live as Territorians in arguably one of the most violent areas on the surface of this earth. If any Territorian were to die because of the actions of a political terrorist we would be alarmed and quick to demand appropriate action be taken by Parliament, the government of the day, the courts and the police. However, daily we witness a carnage far greater in proportion to the terrorism occurring in Northern Ireland. In Central Australia, that is the area to the south of Dunmarra, the annual homicide rate exceeds that for the whole of Victoria in many of the years prior to 1951 and this amongst a population of less than fifty thousand people.'

Despite the early disapprobation of Darwin, the destructive cyclones, the Japanese bombing raids, there has been one thread that has tied the past to the present – the genuine pride of its inhabitants in their city and the fact that they could call themselves Territorians. It has shown itself in many unexpected ways. When, for example, the Northern Territory Government proposed to erect a memorial to commemorate the visit in 1942 of General

Douglas MacArthur to the Batchelor Airstrip, the protests, to the surprise of the politicians, were loud and vociferous. Rather than being hailed as a heroic figure in a gold braid cap, aviator glasses and corncob pipe, poor old Doug got a real pasting. 'Why Dug-out Doug?' questioned the Darwinians, hackles up. 'Why not one of our own blokes?' Trenchant criticism followed. 'Have we so few [local] heroes that we have to build monuments to the likes of Dug-out Doug MacArthur?' asked lawyer and former ALP president, John Waters, echoing the feelings of the populace. 'His earliest military victory was achieved driving tanks against an unarmed ex-servicemen's camp in Washington, DC, in 1932. Against a Japanese force half the size he led the United States Army to its first military defeat since 1812, leaving his soldiers to their fate at Bataan. His obsession to return first victorious to the Philippines cost thousands of Australian lives at Milne Bay, Buna, Finschhafen, Balikpapan and Tarakan.' MacArthur, the lawyer said, was remembered for saying old soldiers never die, they simply fade away. 'We should let his memory do the same.' The controversy snowballed. 'We do not need imported heroes,' one ex-serviceman was quoted in the local newspaper. 'The Australian troops cleaned the Japs from New Guinea and were in Borneo at the war's end. Yet the egomaniac MacArthur saw fit to castigate them for being too slow and too timid.' A monument to Dug-out-Doug was never built, but there was a compromise. The original proposal was watered down and a small plaque signalising MacArthur's arrival in Australia was placed on a rock at the airport.

# Sources

John McKinlay (Explorer), Journal

Douglas Lockwood, *The Front Door*, Darwin 1869-1969, Rigby Limited, 1968

Charles See-Kee, 'Chinese Contribution to Early Darwin', *Occasional Papers No.3*, Northern Territory Library Service 1987

Denis Barritt, 'Some Community Problems from a Court's Perspective' *Occasional Papers No. 26*, State Library of the Northern Territory, 1991

*The Herald*, Melbourne

*The Northern Territory Times*, October 4, 1884

Hugh V Clarke, *The Long Arm: A Biography of a Northern Territory Policeman*, Roebuck Society Publication No 12

C.T.G. Haultain, *Watch Off Arnhem Land*, Roebuck Society Publication No 4

Geoffrey Serle (General Editor), *Australian Dictionary of Biography Vol. 11*, 1891-1939

Syd Kyle-Little, *Whispering Wind – Adventures in Arnhem Land*, Hutchinson of London, 1957

# LAPSES INTO LEVITY

His Worship: 'You have pleaded guilty to stealing a chicken. Have you anything to say?

Defendant: 'Just took it for a bit of a lark, sir.'

His Worship: 'No resemblance whatsoever. Fined fifty dollars.'

'The law,' says Richard Fountain in *The Wit of the Wig* is no less impressive in human terms for the occasional lapse into levity.' A furtive element, he noted, at least of the risible, can occasionally be discerned in our courts.' These 'furtive elements', however, are more likely to occur in the magistrate's courts, where humour, more often than not, is spontaneous, which is the best kind of humour, although clever repartee, too, can enliven an otherwise dull and drawn-out case, as in the following classical exchange that occurred in an English courtroom early last century:

'You will admit,' asked counsel to a medical expert giving evidence, 'that doctors do make mistakes, won't you?

'Yes,' was the reply, 'the same as lawyers.'

'Ah, but doctors' mistakes are buried underground.'

'Yes, but lawyers' mistakes are left swinging in the air.'

Then there was the defendant in a County Court action: 'As God is my judge, I did not take the money.'

Judge: 'He's not, I am, you did.'

But for sheer waspishness, it would be difficult to beat English High Court judge, Sir Melford Stevenson (1902 – 1987) who told an accused: 'I must confess [that] I cannot tell whether you are innocent or guilty. I am giving you three years. If you are guilty, you have got off lightly; if innocent let this be a lesson to you.'

Digressing for a moment, it was back in the reign of King Richard I that the magisterial system originated when, in 1195 and more interested in fighting the infidels than looking after his country, the king appointed the first *Custodes Pacis*, or knights, to maintain law and order in their respective domains. But it was not until one hundred and sixty-six years later, during the reign of Edward III, that these 'keepers of the peace' formally became justices, sitting four times a year 'to hear and determine all manner of felonies and trespasses.' Hence the name Quarter Sessions. In Tudor times, they were jacks-of-all trades, not only responsible for upholding the law, but for bridges, tax enforcement and price regulation as well as prosecuting recusants. By the end of the nineteenth century, many of their non-judicial functions had been lost.

Courts in the Northern Territory have had their fair share of humour. Some years ago, the late Mr C K Ward, stipendiary magistrate, was sitting on a case in the Alice Springs Magistrate's Court when, in a slightly surprised voice, he said to the defendant, 'You have had no less than forty-two convictions for this same offence.' To which the defendant replied: 'Not the SAME offence, yer washup… but, as the barman says when'e arsts if yer wanna 'nother drink – SOMETHINK SIMLAR.

The magistrate made no reply to this and the defendant decided to set the court record even straighter, saying, 'Yair – forty-two convictions is right, and it's taken me forty-two years to get 'em.'

Another defendant pleaded guilty to an assault charge… 'under hixtreme proclamation.' When the court suggested he meant 'provocation, he replied with an injured air, 'Yair, yer Worship, that too and the beggar got me dander up as well.' Proclamation, provocation and 'dander' notwithstanding, he received a five shillings fine and a day to pay.

Bruce McCormack, a magistrate in Darwin in the 80s, who eventually quit the job to study Latin and ancient Greek, was once confronted by a solicitor who pleaded guilty on behalf of a defendant from whom, he assured the court, he had taken 'full instructions.'

'The defendant says he's very, very sorry,' said the solicitor in mitigation of his offence. 'Very, very sorry indeed.'

'How old is he?' asked Mr McCormack.

'One moment, I'll asked my client,' said the solicitor, turning to the man who was sitting behind him. 'He's thirty-two, Your Worship.'

'What does he do for a living?' asked the SM.

'One moment, Your Worship,' said the solicitor, again turning to his client. 'He says he's unemployed, Your Worship.'

'How does he feel about going to jail?

'One moment, Your Worship,' said the solicitor, turning to his 'client' for the third time.

Slowly the solicitor faced the magistrate again, coughed apologetically and said, 'I'm very, very sorry, Your Worship; it seems I've got the wrong defendant.'

The Chief Magistrate around this time was Gerard Galvin who, along with his fellow magistrates, was once referred by the Chief Justice, Sir William Forster, as 'Gerry and the Pacemakers.' Frustrated by the fact that a witness remained silent while he tried to question him, Mr Galvin asked the man's solicitor, Anne Warburton, 'Is he illiterate or something?'

Miss W: 'He's a Queenslander, Your Worship.'

'Ah,' said Mr Galvin, 'that explains it.' (Mr Galvin, admittedly, didn't go as far as another magistrate who, in a different jurisdiction, called a Queenslander 'a clown, an idiot, a ratbag, a nit, a clot and a dickhead.' The Court of Criminal Appeal subsequently ruled that he was not biased!).

Mr Galvin, who later quit to become a teacher in mainland China, was also on the Bench when one Richard Graham Johns, appeared before him clutching a battered old cowboy hat. Without any ado, Richard announced loudly, 'I'm a pioneer, we cut our teeth on rifles up here.' The police prosecutor, Sergeant Nigel McBain, quickly explained that Richard was charged with carrying a loaded rifle while drunk, discharging the gun in a public place and with not having a shooter's licence. It was 4.10 p.m. on Christmas Eve when Richard entered the workshop of the Berrimah Tyre Service and, to the astonishment of an employee, fired a shoot from a Winchester .22 through the tin roof, Sgt McBain said. He then sat down with the rifle between his feet. 'He later told police he had drunk about sixteen cans of beer,' the sergeant said.

'I didn't have 16 cans,' protested the forty-six-year-old Richard. 'Maybe six or eight. I'm not a violent man.'

Mr Galvin, 'But you were drunk?'

Richard, 'Certainly. I had a beer in me and the damn thing went off. That's the honest truth.'

Sgt McBain asked Mr Galvin to order forfeiture of the rifle.

'What do you say to that, Mr Johns?' asked the magistrate.

Richard, 'It's a storm in a tea cup.'

'I take into account there was no malicious intent,' said Mr Galvin, fining Richard four hundred and forfeiting the rifle.

'But it's me mate's gun,' said Richard aghast. 'How am I going to get it back to him?'

But Mr Galvin already had signed the order and Richard, sadly shaking his head, was persuaded to leave the courtroom.

One of the most engaging paradoxes of matrimonial life, that now and again manifests itself in courts of summary jurisdiction, is the way in which husbands, having shed their wives for one reason or another, go through the most dramatic processes to get them back again. Peter, separated from his spouse for a couple of months, was locked in one of these emotional conflicts. And, as often happens, his eloquence fell on stony ears. 'Very well,' he exclaimed before his wife, 'this is the end. Never again shall I appear before you. My blood is on your hands. I shall shoot myself.' With these and sundry other dramatic utterances he strode off into the night, brandishing a .22 rifle. A short time later, two shots rang out, but no harm came to Peter. Far from it. The only serious outcome was that he was charged with discharging a firearm in a public place without lawful excuse. 'He fired a couple of shots into the air,' a detective told the magistrate. 'I have interviewed his wife,' he went on. 'They have been married for six years and have agreed to part for a trial period. He intends, if able, to return to Tasmania by plane this afternoon.' During the hearing Peter, a tall young man, now and again smiled a secret smile to himself as though he had resolved to face the pangs of rejected love with inner fortitude. 'Anything to say?' asked the magistrate. Peter, smiling his little smile, replied, 'No.' So he was promptly fined one hundred and fifty dollars.

During the Daly River Maluk Maluk land claim hearing back in the 1970s the point was raised that there were claims to estates where the clans were thought to be extinct. Contrary to everyone's belief, it turned out that one of the clans wasn't. It was, it was pointed out, incumbent upon the barrister acting for the claimants as he was to try and establish a belief in the claimant people that this particular woman not only was dead but at the time they moved onto the land and assumed responsibilities, had been dead for some time. The barrister, Mr Michael Maurice, was very careful as to the way in which he approached the questions.

He called a senior claimant and asked, 'Did you believe that Kitty Panquee was dead?'

The claimant thought about it for a while and said, 'Yes.'

Mr Maurice, 'Did you think that Kitty Panquee had been dead for a long time or a short time?'

The witness struggled with this question, but eventually brightened and replied, 'Mr Maurice, I thought she was dead for all time.'

In a custody case before Mr Justice Nader in the Supreme Court, Darwin barrister, Mr John Waters, asked his witness, 'Wouldn't you agree that the substance of what you have told us have been a very considerable battle for you, have they not? (sic)' To which the witness replied, 'That's dead right.'

Mr Waters, 'That battle is likely to continue, is it not?'

Witness, 'No, it's not, because you've just heard evidence there that it's been resolved down that I took a single parents' pension to allocate myself to look after the children. At the same time I took that pension, I applied through the pension for a job which would be suitable to look after these children, which subsequently was offered to me at the Darwin Hospital with ongoing benefits to the point, if you work it out, to work for the Public Service, the time you work which is a nine-day fortnight, which leaves for five days a fortnight that you don't work, right, which is ten days a month, which is, by twelve, one hundred and twenty days of the year, right, which is four months of the year for a start, one third of the year that you're not even working, and then you also get six weeks full leave plus two weeks travelling, which is eight weeks, which is another two months, which makes six months. Then you're also entitled to about four weeks sick leave if you're – or four weeks parental leave if the children are in a stage – or you get another four weeks, and then you get another three

45

days extra to attend court if you have to, and then on top of that you can apply for leave without pay. So if you wanted to be a public servant, you needn't have to work at all.'

Mr Waters, 'I thought that was what you were going to say.'

The same judge, in April, 1985, was hearing a family law matter when he addressed Mr Cec Black at the Bar table during, of all things, a debate on unions.

Mr Justice Nader: 'Don't take it too seriously, Mr Black, I know that's how they go on all the time. Haven't you heard the old expression 'muck raking' and all that sort of thing that goes on in the union business all the time? You needn't think that I am going to regard it as any specially (sic) forceful piece of evidence; it is part of the narrative, thought. From time immemorial trade union officials have spent about 90 per cent of their time gathering buckets of foul smelling material to tip on their opponents, and about the other ten per cent attending to their members' interests. That is fairly well accepted, isn't it, Mr Reeves?'

Mr (John) Reeves: 'Has Your Honour taken judicial notice of that? I can't agree – I can't agree with Your Honour.'

Mr Justice Nader: 'What I'm saying is, it doesn't come as a surprise to me and it is true. I will take judicial notice of the fact that in the internecine strife that goes on within unions, officials spend the vast majority of their energies fighting one another and a small part of it preparing logs of claims and going to court and negotiating with the employers, Yes?'

Mr Reeves: 'Well… '

Mr Justice Nader: 'Most of them spend a good deal of time feathering their own nests. If they find that one of their opponents is in a mental ward – I mean, that'd be pennies from heaven. He couldn't expect them not to say something about it – could you?'

Mr Reeves: 'No Your Honour.'

The late Mr Justice William Forster, who spent almost fourteen years in the Territory as a judge, five of which he served as Chief Justice, was a highly regarded jurist and not one to suffer fools gladly. Nor did he mince words. During a voir dire in a murder trial he observed that a certain Crown witness was 'quite devoid of grey matter.' Taking one witness in a civil case to task, he said he was satisfied he had deliberately lied and that his evidence was heavily coloured by his hostility and paranoid suspicion of almost all the solicitors with whom he had contact. On another occasion, obviously displeased by a newspaper article, he referred to the offending publication as 'that wretched paper.'

On the occasion of his official farewell in February, 1985 (he was forced to retire due to ill health) he recalled a witness who told him a number of times that his business was going through a particular 'phrase.'

'When I asked what he meant, he looked at me pityingly, thinking, 'poor, stupid old man',' Sir William said. 'He then replied, 'You know, a particular stage of development.'

Then there was the counsel who asked a witness: 'When you said this occurred after dinner, were you referring to lunch or tea?'

Sir William also recalled the regular confrontations between a Crown prosecutor and 'a certain counsel who is rather small in stature,' so that when he sat on his chair his feet didn't touch the ground. 'The most telling blow,' His Honour said, 'was struck when the prosecutor spoke of his learned friend jumping down to his feet.'

# Sources

*The Wit of the Wig*, compiled by Richard Fountain, Leslie Frewin Publishers Ltd, London, 1968

# THE REVENGE OF
# OLD MA HAWKES

Revenge, according to an English proverb, is a dish that should be eaten cold. Unfortunately, old Mrs Thelma (Ma) Hawkes was in no position to partake of anything, but her ghostly laughter, or croaking, could well have echoed around Paradise, or wherever she was, after she passed away in May, 1981.

For as long as anyone could remember, Ma Hawkes had been the proprietor of the Wanda Inn at Top Springs, a small township on the northern extremity of the Tanami Desert and once described by a defendant who had been arrested there for drunk and disorderly behavior, as about as exciting and cheerful as an empty coffin. A widow rumoured to be exceedingly wealthy, Ma Hawkes suffered a heart attack and died while sitting on the toilet. She was discovered by her Aboriginal houseboy who raised the alarm and told everyone who would listen that in death 'she looked like a frog.' The nearest police station was at Wave Hill now known as Kalkaringi and Constable Kevin Dailly, being the only policeman stationed there at the time, was directed to attend, take possession of the deceased's assets and initiate any other 'appropriate action.' Jumping into the police four-wheel drive vehicle, PC Dailly quickly covered the hundred and sixty kilometres from the Aboriginal settlement to Top Springs. On arrival, he made arrangements for the care of the body, went through Ma Hawkes' belongings and diligently collected all her valuables. He also duly reported to his senior officer, Sgt Paddy McQuade, officer-in-charge at Katherine, that there were no suspicious circumstances surrounding the death. The following day, the Public Trustee, Mr John Flynn, and his deputy arrived from Darwin and PC Dailly promptly handed them fifty-two thousand dollars in cash as well as a quantity of expensive jewellery, including a diamond ring worth fifteen thousand dollars. 'I can't say other than that he was most helpful and co-operative, outstandingly so,' Mr Flynn later recalled. The sworn valuation of the total estate for probate, he added, was two hundred and twenty-seven thousand, seven hundred and twenty-eight dollars. However, apparently PC Dailly failed to hand over to the Trustee another twenty-eight thousand, five hundred and fifty dollars in cash which he had found hidden in Ma Hawkes' house and which he took back to Wave Hill and buried in the yard of the police station. And there it remained until exactly seven months later when an Aboriginal police tracker who was watering fruit trees in the yard, saw PC Dailly's dog, Len (named after Sergeant Len Pryce, who, at the time was officer-in-charge at Katherine), chasing a frog which jumped into a hole. Pouncing on the hole, the dog started to try and dig out his quarry. It was then, much to the tracker's astonishment, that one dollar, five dollar and ten dollar notes began to surface, for the frog had picked the same hole in which PC Dailly had buried the stolen money. As the dog kept scrabbling, more and more notes began appearing. And at that precise moment a willy willy swept across the yard, sending them swirling into the air. The tracker scurried off to tell the officer who was then in charge of Wave Hill, Senior Constable Bob Bruce. Initial disbelief was quickly dispelled when he saw that the yard was literally littered with notes. Not without difficulty, for some of the money had been blown across the settlement, Snr Const Bruce retrieved the money and when PC Dailly later came on duty, he taxed him about it.

At first he denied all knowledge of the cash, but later, when questioned by senior officers who arrived from Darwin, he made, as the police cutely put it, 'full and frank admissions.'

After the Chief Magistrate, Mr Gerard Galvin, found a prima facie case against Dailly, the constable, pleading guilty to larceny, came up for sentence before His Honour, Mr Justice John Gallop, in the Northern Territory Supreme Court. Maintaining a poker face, the judge recited the bizarre facts that led to PC Dailly's arraignment. In the scale of larceny as a public servant, he said, the offence committed by the accused loomed large and grave. 'Not only did he succumb to the temptation to take the money, but he furtively hid it and perpetuated the breach of trust. His crime was only discovered accidentally. I am told it is inevitable that he will be dismissed from the police force with all the disgrace and dishonour appropriate to that dismissal. There are strong grounds for leniency, but I believe that the general public would expect a custodial sentence to be imposed in the circumstances of this case as a general lesson to police officers, or other public servants who have committed breach of trust reposed in them by their office, and sustain that breach for a long time.'

PC Dailly was sentenced to two years' jail, but the judge directed he be released after serving six months on him entering a two-year good behaviour bond.

And back at Wave Hill, the Aborigines were in no doubt that the frog was the spirit of old Ma Hawkes and that she had finally got her revenge.

# SUNSHINE'S OFFER

The late Mr Justice James Muirhead was a charitable and humane judge. One of the doyens of the legal world, he was unfailingly courteous in court and no one was ever heard to say a harsh, or critical, word about him. Born in Adelaide in 1925, he served with the infantry in the Pacific during the Second World War. His legal career began when he entered the Adelaide Bar in 1950 as an ambitious twenty-five-year-old. In 1974 he was appointed as the second residential judge in the Northern Territory, joining Mr Justice Forster. Then, in 1987, he was appointed head of the Aboriginal Deaths in Custody Commission. Fourteen months later he stepped down as head of the commission – the work, he said, had been 'emotionally pretty wearing and initially very, very difficult' – and was appointed Administrator of the Northern Territory.

During his time as judge of the Territory Supreme Court, a white prostitute was arraigned before him charged with the murder of a man who had been an alcoholic derelict – a man who had previously attempted suicide with a knife. Pending her trial, the judge released her on bail on the condition that she place herself under some type of care. She ended up at the YWCA of which the judge's wife, Margaret, was the executive director – 'not an ideal arrangement,' the judge later observed. Pending her trial, she was cared for by one of the staff. At the outset, she pleaded not guilty and was defended by Mr John Coombe Q.C., a member of the NSW Bar. His client was a diminutive woman who, as her trial progressed, continually interrupted proceedings with loud comments while Crown witnesses were giving their evidence. She had a special dislike for one particular bespectacled detective who she persisted in calling 'Mr

Fuckin' Four Eyes,' until the judge patiently asked her to keep quiet.

It was, the judge was later to remark, an extraordinary trial. It was common ground that when the police arrived at the alleged murder scene – in a room in a run-down boarding house in Darwin's Mitchell Street – the man was dead and lying on a bed with a knife in his chest. The accused, who was later referred to by the judge as 'Sunshine,' was 'observed' attempting to hammer the knife further in with the heel of one of her shoes. She was 'very, very drunk.'

The accuracy of the initial police observations were not challenged, but 'Sunshine,' in an unsworn statement from the dock, professed no memory at all of the events. As the jury listened spellbound, she then launched on a lurid story of her life.

The jury, at the conclusion of her mitigating address that was liberally sprinkled with four letter words, evidently felt sorry for her and she was acquitted.

Some years later, the judge penned a sequel to the story in his autobiography, 'A Brief Summing Up,' which he wrote not long before his death.

After her trial, Sunshine had her ups and downs and Margaret [Mrs Muirhead] did what she could to help her. Some time later, as I was walking past a hotel in Darwin, she emerged. Clearly she had consumed a few drinks.

'Hello, Judge,' she said, 'How are you?

'Fine,' I replied.

'Judge,' she said, 'I guess I owe you one.

'Don't talk like that, Sunshine,' I replied.

'No,' she said in a contemplative manner. 'It wouldn't be fair to Mrs Muirhead, would it?'

'Only a few trials in the criminal court were vaguely amusing,' Judge Muirhead wrote in his autobiography.

I recall a young woman and three or four men charged with an assault occasioning actual bodily harm. The victim hailed from Yugoslavia – a huge man and, I think, a miner by occupation. His lifestyle was to work out in the bush for weeks, accumulate plenty of cash and then to enjoy himself for a few days in Darwin where he stayed at a cheap boarding house not far from the original site of the Darwin Casino. On the night in question his gambling had paid handsomely. He returned to his room and telephoned a call girl service, particularly requesting a 'big, fat blonde.' The girl arrived, but she was slim and dark. He complained, but she told him she was the only girl available. Time and price were negotiated; but he was not pleased but he utilised her services. Later she told him 'time was up' and asked for more money. He was furious and propelled her out of the door with no money at all.

A short time later she returned with three or four minders. He had anticipated such a visit. Believing that offence was the best firm of defence, he charged out with great velocity, scattering all and sundry. I think one minder was thrown down the stairs of the landing adjacent to his room. But the numbers prevailed and he was felled by an iron bar. In the meantime the girl entered the room and extracted her fee from his wallet including, I suspect, her overtime allowance. What I recall about the case is principally the man's answers in cross-examination by defence counsel. He was voluble and found it impossible to answer 'yes' or 'no.' It was put to him that he first became angry when a blonde did not arrive, with which he heartedly agreed, but he put his answer something like this: 'Mr M,' he asked the Defence counsel, 'do you like pork or beef?'

'I told the witness that he could not question Counsel in this manner. 'Well,' he said, 'some people like beef, but some people prefer pork. I eat them both, but I just like big fat blondes. That's why I asked for one. Of course I was angry'.

'It was one of those few cases when I sat with a jury the members of which appeared to thoroughly enjoy it all.

Judge Muirhead's compassion was shown in another homicide, the setting of which was the tranquil surroundings of the Adelaide River War Cemetery. During the Second World War, Adelaide River was the headquarters of a large base and the war cemetery was established for the burial of servicemen and women who died in northern hospitals. After the war, the Army Graves Service moved graves from civil cemeteries, isolated sites and temporary military burial grounds to the Adelaide cemetery. During the 1970s the four hundred and thirty-four graves were looked after by the curator, Tom Scales who, with his wife, Martha (not their real names) lived in apparent peaceful harmony in a house in the grounds.

Tom was a small, thin, sharp-faced man who seemed to get along with everyone. But behind his bonhomie there lurked a dark side – he was a wife beater. During their married years Tom treated Martha cruelly, beating her and sometimes tying her to her bed and abusing her. Martha bore it stoically until one evening this mild-tempered woman snapped. As Tom was watching TV, a towel covering his waist, she armed herself with a knife, crept up behind him and plunged it into his chest. Police later found him with his hand, set in rigor mortis, clutched over the handle. So hard had the knife been thrust into his heart that the investigating sergeant, Harry Cox, a strong, burly man, was unable to pull it out. Martha, in the meantime, ran to a nearby house and gave herself up. Arraigned before Judge

Muirhead, she pleaded not guilty to murder but guilty to manslaughter. The Crown accepted the lesser plea.

During the trial Martha sat in the dock with her head bowed. The facts weren't disputed and in his summing up the judge emphasised the abuse she had suffered. The jury found her guilty. However, because of her previous good character and the fact that he was sure she would never re-offend, he released her on a three-year good behaviour bond. Martha walked out of the courtroom a free woman. But she had only one thing in mind. She walked across to the Darwin police station which, at that time, was located almost opposite the courthouse and asked the desk sergeant, Sgt Jack Nichol, if she could have her knife back (the police had kept it as evidence). It was, she explained, her favourite carving knife.

James Muirhead died during a visit to Darwin in July 1999. He was deeply mourned.

## Sources

J H Muirhead, *A Brief Summing Up*, Access Press, 1966

# LINDY AND THE
# UNPUBLISHED FILES

The decade of the 1980s saw Australia experiencing a unique social phenomenon. Suddenly, lounge room lawyers popped up all over the country, in every town and city. Some were for the defence but most, mainly women, were for the prosecution. They all had their own opinion – without seeking to know the facts. Myths and misinformation abounded. Heated arguments were common. Newsletters were published. People became obsessed. Many 'knew' the accused woman was guilty because she didn't display any outward emotion. She didn't break down and cry. It was a trial by public opinion. Dr Norman Young, a Seventh Day Adventist theologian, in his book Innocence Regained wrote that 'instead of protecting [the accused] from the public prejudice, the law became part of it.'

The event that sparked this bizarre episode in Australia's legal history was, of course, the Chamberlain trial. It was an extraordinary case, yet when all boiled down it was simply one of a missing baby with the unusual name of Azaria.

Now this is not a rehash of the trials of that much-portrayed woman, Lindy, charged with the murder of her baby, or of the trial of her former husband Michael. This chapter comprises material that has not been published. My own association with the Chamberlain case began on the morning of August 17, 1980, at the regular daily police conference in Darwin when, after reading through the running sheets, Sergeant Daryl Manzie (who, ironically, later became Attorney-General of the Northern Territory), said to the three or four journalists present: 'Well, the only thing that might interest you is that a dingo has taken a baby at Ayers Rock.' The story was filed to southern newspapers and the saga, 'estimated to cost between twenty and seventy million dollars', began.

After the trial Michael Chamberlain, who had been found guilty of being accessory after the fact, made a surprise call to my home and we talked for some time. What were my feelings about the trial? he asked. It was an unexpected question but I remember replying that counsel for the prosecution, Ian Barker, completely upstaged counsel for the defence, John Phillips QC (later to become Chief Justice of Victoria). The Chamberlains had chosen the wrong lawyer. They had needed a much more flamboyant barrister to counteract Barker.

Then, not so long ago, during a visit to Darwin, I was handed three large files that had been locked away in a lawyer's safe. The files, containing hundreds of letters to Attorney-General Manzie, about the case, reveal the emotional involvement, bordering on hysteria, which it evoked. One letter came from as far away as Penscola in Florida, several came from Canada. God was invoked dozens of times. The Bible was quoted, even Rudyard Kipling. Some were disjointed and rambling. Other writers obviously had no knowledge of the law. Much was defamatory. One writer following the case likened it to an 'extraordinary walk with the Lord' which had resulted in 'incredible strain.' An eighteen page hand written letter written by a 'Biblical scholar' from New Zealand, listed what he perceived as the 'evils' of the Seventh Day Adventist Church (to which the Chamberlains belonged), and confessed he had 'quickly become very unpopular with them because of my ability to expose them.' 'I trust,' he told The Secretary, Department of Law, to whom the letter was addressed, 'that this information will be of use to you.' An accompanying note to Prosecutions simply said 'good one.'

The case seemed to dominate some people's lives. Wrote one woman, 'Last year I gave up everything in my life to intercede for this case. It was a rough time for me all round because in that time I was living solely one a supporting parent's income which was downright difficult.' How she 'gave up everything' she didn't explain, but she did concede it had become 'an extremely emotional issue with me.' Another woman wrote: 'I have followed the case very closely and never wavered in my belief that she was innocent.' And again, from a 'seventy-year-old war vet', 'These are my thoughts – and I will have them till I die.' The law of defamation prevent his thoughts from being published.

In 1988, following the exoneration of Lindy and Michael by the Morling Commission, the Northern Territory Court of Criminal Appeal quashed their convictions. The matter of compensation then arose.

What the Chamberlains were entitled to was the subject of many letters and aroused strong feelings. One, from a group of Chamberlain supporters, began: 'Thank you Mr Manzie for refusing to consider the Chamberlains' claim for compensation. We love to hate you bastards. Because we know Lindy will become more than more famous and revered world-wide while you miserable scum will become more and more despised.' It continued in the same vein. Another sought the Lord's advice: 'I noticed in the paper that the Chamberlains had applied for four million dollars in compensation! I keep praying and seeking the Lord in this and He clearly states that they will not receive compensation.' Clearly, the Lord was mistaken. The Northern Territory Government finally paid the Chamberlains one million, three hundred thousand dollars plus three hundred and ninety-six dollars for legal costs and nineteen thousand dollars for their dismembered car.

Some writers even went so far as threatening never to visit the Territory, or, in one instance, to leave the country. One man was so incensed with what he believed was the Territory Government's ill-treatment of the Chamberlains, after their convictions were quashed that he wrote: 'I personally am afraid to enter the NT' while another, in criticising the Government's delay in paying compensation to the Chamberlains, said: 'It is dirty mean and I will leave it at that.' Nevertheless, he went on: 'I will not be long here in Australia. It has no future. I will return to Ireland which has.' And another: 'We look forward to hearing… that men and women need not be afraid to visit your area for fear of misjustice (sic) by the government.'

A letter from Ontario, Canada, said until the Northern Territory Government paid compensation to the Chamberlains 'on a matter of principal (sic) I must state that neither 'foot nor farthing' shall touch your fair land until the matter is concluded.' In a separate letter to 'the Minister of Trade and Commerce, Northern Territory', the same writer said: 'We are embarking on a boycott of any Australian goods and are encouraging our friends to do the same until the Chamberlains have received the compensation they request.'

Some correspondents began their letters in a rather roundabout way before broaching the subject of the Chamberlains. Addressed to 'the Chief Administrator and all Parliamentarians of the Northern Territory in Parliament Assembled,' and headed 'Issue – the Chamberlain Case' the writer commenced:

> Long before man came out of the cave and invented the art of writing, and subsequently printing and discovered how to make paper, and formulated laws and founded Law Schools and established courts to ensure the implementation of the law, THE LAW of preservation of the offspring of all living creatures on the planet existed – that is a UNIVERSAL LAW that is infused in all living creatures, be it man, mammal, reptile, bird etc etc. Note how the Kangaroo to preserve its helpless young, carries it in its pouch until it can look after itself.

The writer went on to describe how various animals cared for their young, citing, in doing so, Christ, Confusius (sic) and Mohammed.

Animals aside, one writer thought the discovery of a sock would be of interest to the government. 'I read an interesting article in a paper recently regarding the finding of a Viking sock centuries old,' he told Mr Manzie. '[It was] found in the very cold snowy regions somewhere, the sock was very well preserved.'

One woman sought a higher office to send her letter. Not only was she sending her letter to Mr Manzie, she wrote, but she was also going to present it to Her Majesty. It was an anti-Chamberlain letter.

A correspondent who objected to the Chamberlains being paid compensation attached a cutting, possibly from a magazine, to his letter: 'Dog days date from July 3 to August 11, covering a period of 40 days when Sirius, or the dog star, rises and sets with the sun. The ancient superstition was that this star exercised direct influence over the canine race.' What this had to do with compensation wasn't explained.

'This side of Eternity,' wrote one, 'it will be very hard to compensate the Chamberlains for all their needless suffering...' While another, opposing any payment, wrote: 'It nearly made my blood boil when I saw them in TV.' The writer signed her letter with 'Regards, God bless you richly.' And from a supporter: 'They have suffered enough. It has been a modern crucification (sic). The intelligent ones of us knew that they didn't commit the crimes they were accused of.'

One woman from NSW was somewhat critical of the appeal itself. She felt compelled to air her feelings. To Mr Manzie she wrote:

> My opinion is the [Morling] inquiry was a bit of a circus. The Defence witnesses were very eccentric people and some were decidedly barmy. I've never

heard more incredible ramblings (and that's the only way to describe them) as uttered by a Dr Pluekahn from Melbourne Hospital. He was actually calling L Chamberlain as being 'like a beam of light' and the last straw was calling her the reincarnation of Joan of Arc. Another witness from a Japanese institution (he was English); honestly I've never heard such convoluted, disjointed dialogue that could have been hysterically funny if one did not think about him being allowed to waffle on such rubbish at the taxpayers' expense.

And as for Mr Justice Morling, 'he permitted the most astounding display of tantrums.' And on the letter went – three closely hand-written pages.

After sending at least half a dozen letters to Mr Manzie, one woman still couldn't dismiss the case from her mind. 'Dear Daryl,' she wrote, obviously feeling that after all her correspondence she could address the Attorney-General by his given name, 'I felt to write and let you know that the Chamberlain case is still heavily upon me.' (And this was eight years after the trial).

Included in one of the files was a submission on assessment of compensation delivered to Mr Justice Morling by the Chamberlains' solicitor, Mr S Tipple. A couple of the paragraphs are worth quoting:

> The 'media circus' has been an inevitable and inexorable consequence of the factual cocktail which has surrounded Azaria's death. By the time of the first inquest [in Alice Springs when the Coroner, Denis Barritt, now deceased, found death by dingo] these facts had become of such intense public interest that the most defamatory inferences and innuendoes had been drawn against the Chamberlains and had already commenced to circulate about them. If anything was calculated to ensure that the Chamberlains

> were to be indelibly engraved in the public mind it
> was [the decision] to take Azaria's clothing to London
> and to put it into the hands of a person who was short-
> ly thereafter proclaimed by the Northern Territory to
> be a 'foremost world expert,' followed by a decision to
> publicly proclaim that the case was being 're-opened.'
> The incontrovertible fact is that... the Northern
> Territory believed that the matter should be pursued
> and they pursued it with such vigour that eventually
> convictions were secured, which convictions later
> events have shown to have been unjust.

A leading article in the Australian Law Journal that appeared after the trial said that the prosecution case led by Ian Barker had brought about the verdict rather than the circumstantial evidence that was presented.

In 1987, a year before the Morling inquiry, the Northern Territory Government amended its Criminal Code by inserting the following: 'Where... a person has been convicted of a crime or an indictable offence and the prerogative of mercy has been extended to the person in respect of that conviction, the Attorney-General may, at the request of the convicted person, if the Attorney-General is satisfied that it is expedient in the interests of justice to do so, refer the case to the Court to enable the Court to consider or again consider whether the conviction should be quashed and a judgement and verdict of acquittal entered.'

# Sources

Estimation of cost of seven separate legal inquiries into the disappearance of Azaria, article by Heath Gilmore, *Sun-Herald*, July 30, 2000

# WURRAN AND THE SPIRIT DOG

In her initial years as Darwin's first woman magistrate, and first woman stipendiary magistrate in Australia, Sally Thomas (later to become Chief Magistrate of the Northern Territory and then a Supreme Court judge) had more than her fair share of Aboriginal ghosts and spirits. In fact, if ever there was a ghost hovering around, it always seemed to end up in Sally's lap. One case involved the ghost of an Aboriginal elder who had more than twenty wives, and another the spirit of a dog that was looking after a missing four-year-old girl. In both cases Sally was acting as coroner.

Little Wurran Two disappeared on Howard Island off the coast of Arnhem Land in 1982. The island is very arid. On the eastern side there is low thick scrub and on the western and south western side is a heavy seawater swamp. Members of Wurran's tribe had been reluctant search for her because they had seen the black spirit dog and they knew it was looking after her.

A report tendered to the coroner related the known facts. Wurran had tailed after her aunt when she set out to go hunting for turtles. The aunt had travelled only a short way when, noticing Wurran was following, told her to go back to the camp. Later, when she returned to the camp it was discovered that Wurran was missing. The next day members of the police task force and Army Reserve, accompanied by an Aboriginal police aide, arrived on the island and began searching. They were told that Wurran's mother and aunt had found where the child had been digging holes with a stick, but, oddly, no tracks had been located. A line search that included twenty-five Aborigines was organised but no trace of the child was found. Two days later the search was resumed, but it became obvious to the police that the Aborigines were most reluctant to take part in the physical aspects of the search. They said the girl had been taken by the spirit of her grandmother who had died two months previously in Milingimbi, and that she was a good spirit and would return the child when she was ready.

At the same time the story of a spirit dog came to light. Wurran's father, James Two, had shot a black dog on Howard Island a short time previously for biting another child. He had returned later to dispose of the dog's body and found it missing. Aborigines at the camp said that the spirit of the dog was travelling with the girl and looking after her. This became relevant in relation to later sightings of dogs and dog tracks. Meanwhile, Aborigines in the search required constant supervision to keep them involved and even then, many managed to slip away and leave the line search pattern. Aborigines at the camp, spoken to at considerable length, were adamant that one day when the spirit had finished with Wurran she would be returned. Wurran's father, asked about the possibility of pay-back, said it did not happen in this day with the Milingimbi people and if it did occur he would have been told about it.

Although police scoured the island, assisted by an aerial search, there was no confirmed sighting of a dog travelling with Wurran. The country was very demanding on the ground parties, so the Coroner was told, the terrain ranging from wet swamp to dry ironstone country, while the only fresh water available to drink was located in the swamp. If Wurran had left the area of the swamp she would have perished in the dry ironstone country. And if she died in the swamp, the police were confident that the line search parties would have found her. The location of birds circling was investigated with negative results.

For seven days the entire coastline and beach area of Howard Island was covered by helicopter, and by ground search and if Wurran had managed to walk out of the bush she would have been found.

The spirit never returned Wurran to her family. She disappeared without trace. Sally Thomas was 'unable to make any findings as to the cause of death.'

When the Darwin casino at Mindil Beach was being built, Coroner Sally Thomas was told that the area under and around the site was an Aboriginal burial ground and a sacred site. The most famous grave was that of Turimpi, a Tiwi elder. Turimpi's final resting place had been positively identified on the boundary of the beach side of the casino. A powerful man who used to swim and walk from Bathurst Island to Darwin at low tide, he was known to have had more than twenty wives.

Turimpi's name cropped up during an inquiry into the finding in 1977 and 1978 of skeletal remains on the beach while preparatory work on the casino was being done. And the inquiry was warned Turimpi might well haunt the casino if his bones were disturbed. Anthropologist David Ritchie, who appeared for the Tiwi Larrakeyah and Wagaidj clans, said a large number of burials had taken place at the beach between 1913 and 1939. And more bones were likely to be found if more holes were dug.

At the time of the burials, the area had been isolated from Darwin by jungle and swamps. Bodies from the Kahlin Aboriginal compound were taken to the beach by canoe. The compound was established in 1913 and Aborigines from camps around Darwin were forced to live there. Mr Ritchie said there were differences of opinion about the extent of the area in which the burials took place. Some people believed the graves to be on the casino site, while others maintained the whole foreshore had been used.

After adjourning the inquiry for several months, Mrs Thomas found that the bones were, indeed Aboriginal remains and there had been no suggestion of foul play. The warning about Turimpi's ghost didn't, of course, deter Federal Hotels from building their casino. But the story gained its own myth. It was said that his ghost, followed by one of his wives, would be seen on the night of the full moon. And if anyone saw the apparition it would bring bad luck and they would surely lose their money at the casino. Not surprisingly, no one ever confessed to a sighting.

# THE ABDUCTION OF NOLA BROWN

It was probably the first move to reverse a policy that had resulted in what became known as the stolen children generation. It involved a future Minister for Foreign Affairs, the police, two pioneering lawyers, a Harry Lime character, a respected white couple, a disqualified pilot and a seven-year-old part Aboriginal girl, Nola Brown.

It was 1973, a watershed year for Aborigines in the Territory. It was the year that Justice Woodward made his first report on Aboriginal land claims after being appointed Royal Commissioner by the new Federal Labor Government. The inquiry was limited to the Northern Territory because Prime Minister Whitlam believed the Commonwealth's jurisdiction there over Aboriginal affairs could not be successfully challenged. Twenty-five years later, more than half the land in the Territory had been successfully claimed, or was subject of pending claims. The Federal Minister for Aboriginal Affairs, Gordon Bryant, was also establishing a committee to advise on race relations. It was the year that John Nelson, son of Harold Nelson, union leader of the 1918 bloodless rebellion in Darwin that had ousted the Administrator, was appointed Administrator. It was also the year that plans were being made to hold Darwin's first Beer Can Regatta, the brain-child of a wine quaffing Irishman, Paul Rice Chapman, and a local businessman, Lutz Frankenfeld. And later that year, Nola Brown was kidnapped.

Nola had been living a harmonious existence with white foster parents, Mr and Mrs Athol Brown, in Rapid Creek, a suburb of Darwin. A premature baby, she had been fostered out to the Browns shortly after her birth at the Darwin Hospital. Her natural mother was a full blood Aboriginal from Maningrida and was separated from Nola's father. The then Department of Aboriginal Affairs had assumed the care and control of the baby and had duly processed the subsequent placement of the child with the Browns. For the next seven years Nola grew up in a totally white environment. She attended the local Rapid Creek Primary School and had no contact with her Aboriginal mother or siblings living at the coastal settlement at Maningrida.

In early September, while visiting her thirteen-year-old brother, Leo at the Bagot Aboriginal settlement, Nola was approached by a group of men, bundled into a car, and driven to Darwin Airport. It is not known whether she resisted or attempted to flee her abductors. At the airport, a twin engine Cessna light aircraft had been arranged to fly Nola back to her natural mother at Maningrida. She was accompanied by two of her abductors and the pilot, a well-known Darwin identity, John Gabriel who, at the time, was disqualified from flying by the Department of Civil Aviation for various breaches. Nola was never to see her white foster parents again.

The distraught Browns, upon discovering Nola's disappearance, immediately notified the police. However, before the police could intervene they were told by representatives of the North Australian Aboriginal Legal Aid Service (NAALAS) that the youngster had been lawfully returned to her natural mother and were warned not to interfere. In the days that followed, Nola's seizure was to make headlines and bring into place a chain of events that would affect the lives of all the individual people connected with the event.

The North Australian Aboriginal Legal Aid Service, which was to claim full responsibility for the funding and implementation of the abduction, was governed by a six-man executive council. Apart from two white solicitors, who had set up the legal side of the service (it had been established the previous year by the Labor Government), all its employees, including four field officers, were part

Aborigines. The service was the first of its type in Australia in that it was to be a totally autonomous Aboriginal-run legal organisation. It was allocated a substantial grant from the government with no, or little, constraints as to how such funding was to be applied.

The six-man executive council was designed to be representative of the main Aboriginal settlements throughout the Territory. Its director and chairman, Bill Ryan, who was also the president, was a part Aborigine taken from his full blood Aboriginal mother at birth and exiled to Croker Island by the then Administrator. Ryan, together with a government social worker, John Tomlinson, played a major role in Nola's abduction. Ryan was something of an enigma. Associates saw him as a Harry Lime figure, a tall, striking man, quietly spoken, appearing and then disappearing and invariably maintaining an aloof attitude.

It was probably as a result of his upbringing that he became a very private, brooding man who was reluctant to discuss his background. Little was known of him other than that his time on Croker Island was to have an impact upon him in later life. Like so many part Aboriginal children of his time, Ryan was taken by arrangement and under the full authority of the then Administrator, to Croker Island, a remote island off the northern coast of Australia. The island was designated as a settlement for illegitimate Aboriginal children and was governed by a superintendent, Rupert Kentish, who later became a prominent member of the ruling Country-liberal Party in the Legislative Assembly, and who, according to all the evidence available, ruled with an iron fist.

Like all other unwanted part Aboriginal children at the time Ryan endured many years of extreme deprivation and humiliation at the hands of Kentish. One form of Kentish's discipline included shaving the heads of young females who had incurred his wrath and then banishing them to a sandbar for days on end without food or water. Ryan himself hardly ever spoke about his early years on Croker, but one incident he never forgot. To punish Ryan for a minor misdemeanour, Kentish killed his pet horse by pole-axing it while the horrified youngster looked on. It was to be in his later role as President of NAALAS that Ryan was to have the capacity and financial means to seek to right the wrongs of his own haunted past.

Although Nola's abduction was to bring about the intended public attention to the wrongs of taking Aboriginal children from their natural mothers, it also created ill-feeling and distrust among the key participants in the exercise. It put in motion events that would affect not only the foster parents but all of those connected with NAALAS.

The two white solicitors engaged by the service were to threaten a walk-out on the basis that Ryan and his accomplices had abused the Legal Service Charter and had involved the service in improper and potentially illegal activities. They took the view that the identification of the service with the abductors by association implicated them in an unlawful act and threatened to resign unless and until NAALAS removed itself from involvement in the abduction.

The solicitors subsequently were to appear on local ABC TV to lambast the role of NAALAS in the abduction. They also issued a writ against the local newspaper, the NT News, alleging that an article it had published about the abduction had implicated the solicitors in an unlawful act. (The matter was finally settled out of court, the News agreeing to donate the one thousand dollars in damages to the Salvation Army). At the same time, the then Chief Magistrate, David McCann, offered the service solicitors all the support of the judiciary that was necessary to ensure their continued role in representing Aborigines before the Darwin courts.

It was at this stage that the special advisor to the then Aboriginal Affairs Department, Gareth Evans, who would later become Minister for Foreign Affairs, entered the scene. One evening shortly after the solicitors threatened to resign

Evans, who had made a special trip from Canberra, invited them for drinks at the city's well-known watering hole, the Vic Hotel. At the meeting he made it clear to the solicitors that the use and involvement of NAALAS funds in the adduction of Nola was not their business and to 'pull their heads in,' to use his blunt phrase. He was not in any way interested in the use or alleged misuse of funds allocated to the service. It was a matter for the Aboriginal community alone to utilise the funds in any way it saw fit. The two solicitors subsequently resigned. One went intro private practice and the other joined the Australian Legal Aid Service.

The return of Nola outraged white opinion in the Territory, but in southern states, a more reflective view was taken. As a result several reviewed their Aboriginal foster placements. Aboriginal Affairs Minister, Gordon Bryant, also ordered the fostering and adoption policy to be changed so that Aboriginal children could only be fostered or adopted into Aboriginal families, but the policy was interpreted by officers of the Adoption Section of the Community Welfare Division only to refer to children of total descent. Nevertheless, the Division phased out its Part Aboriginal Southern Adoption Scheme – the major exporting source of children of Aboriginal descent to southern states.

After joining her mother in Maningrida, Nola Brown Bambiaga moved to a homeland outstation where she married a member of her tribe. Bill Ryan, because of his 'intimate' involvement in Nola's abduction, subsequently was sacked from his position in the service and, according to a colleague, 'vanished into the oblivion he initially came from.' John Tomlinson, the government social worker (more of whom later) was found guilty on a number of charges relating to Nola's abduction, including disobeying an instruction from Aboriginal Affairs Minister Bryant, failing to give effect to the instruction and improper conduct insomuch as he made false written statements to the department about the case. He was downgraded from an acting class three social worker to a class one, a demotion, it was pointed out, that would cost him at least sixty thousand dollars in salary and increments during the next thirty years.

The process of returning Aboriginal children to their own families was painfully slow and every time an attempt was made, there was considerable white resistance. Understandably, foster parents and mission authorities running institutions had grown attached to the youngsters and, of course, stood to lose the foster payment. But the Nola Brown case undoubtedly marked the beginning of change. A little over two years later the first national conference on adoption was held in Sydney, attended by Aborigines and white welfare officials. It set out a recommendation which read, in part:

> Any Aboriginal child growing up in Australian society today will be confronted by racism. His best weapons against entrenched prejudice are a pride in his Aboriginal identity and cultural heritage, and strong support from other members of the Aboriginal community. We believe that the only way in which an Aboriginal child who is removed from the care of his parents can develop a strong identity and learn to cope with racism is through placement in an environment which reinforces the social and cultural values characteristic of Aboriginal society. We believe that white families are unable to provide such a supportive environment... placement of Aboriginal children (whether for adoption or foster care) should be the sole prerogative of the Aboriginal people. Criteria relating to material possessions and wealth are no substitute for love, pride in the Aboriginal identity and relationships with other Aborigines in the black community.

# EARLY TALES OF GOING TROPPO

There was a common saying that during the wet season half of Darwin's population go troppo and the other half leave. It was, of course, rather an exaggeration, but idiosyncrasies did surface now and then. One such literally hopped up when police received a call from a resident complaining about frogs croaking at night in a nearby paddock. With what must have been a resigned sigh, the duty sergeant asked the night patrol to investigate. Finding the complainant was not at home, the night patrolmen spoke to neighbours who confirmed the complaint. Police on day shift were directed to pursue the matter and to politely explain to the complainant that, due to pressure of work, there would be no time to attend to the frogs. Nevertheless they were asked to tell the complainant that they were being issued with size a hundred and thirty-two gumboots for the following night.

The next reference to the frogs appeared as an entry in the duty book: 'Day shift advise attending and ascertained that the main offender in this matter is known as Freddo, described as big, fat and green. Inquiries reveal he is the ring-leader and has been inciting other frogs to croak. It is believed that if he is removed the problem will be solved. However, this is a matter for the Stock Squad.'

Whether the Stock Squad was told is not known. But one final entry appeared: 'Sergeant Geoff Preston (Task Force) called in re siege of frogs. Riot Squad called out. Ambulance in attendance. Fire brigade water cannon used to disperse frogs. Eighteen arrests. Freddo charged with causing a substantial annoyance.' Apparently there were no more complaints about frogs after that.

Meantime, back at Northern Command, Number One Division Police District, Constable Lancelot John Irving, was diligently recording a conversation he had with one Dominico Ginondo, 'aged about thirty-five.'

'At about 5.45 a.m., I was on uniform patrol in company with Constable P Gleeson when I saw a green and white panel van parked in the car park at the end of Stokes Hill Wharf,' wrote Constable Irving. 'I approached this vehicle but when I got within two metres of it a large white dog ran out from underneath it, barking loudly. It ran to the end of its chain but continually snapped and barked at me. This chain was connected to the rear of the panel van. The noise awoke a person sleeping inside the van and he approached me. In company with Constable Gleeson, I had the following conversation with this person.

'Is that dog registered?' indicating the dog.

'Yes, yes. It run out November 30 this year.'

'When did you register the dog?'

'November 30 last year. For 12 month.'

'All dog registrations run out on the 30th June on the end of the fiscal year.'

'No, you tell fucking lie. 30 November for twelve month I register him. For one year.'

'It's not like car registration. All dog registrations expire on the 30th June following their issue.'

'You tell fucking lie. I love the law. You tell fucking lie. That dog, he registered for one year. 30 November.'

'You had better check with the council over the expiry date.

'You fucking check. This dog registered. I no go to council. You get fucked. You fucking lie.'

'I've told you. It's not like car registration.'

'You tell fucking lie.'

'Get the tag off the dog and bring it here.' This he did and handed me a triangular dog tag for District 20. The expiry date was unreadable.

'What type of dog is it?'

'Big dog.'

'Was that 'big' or 'pig'?'

'Big.'

'A check will be made with the council and you may receive a summons for owning an unregistered dog. Do you understand that?'

'Is registered.'

'The conversation then concluded,' the constable added.

If frogs and dogs weren't enough to test a policeman's patience, there was also the case of Quaxter, a normally placid duck who went about her business like any other duck. But one Sunday (also during the wet season) she became so belligerent that a resident complained to police that a savage duck was attacking people in the Darwin suburb of Malak. A squad car was sent to the area and Quaxter's owner was tracked down. There was, she patiently explained, a perfectly simple reason for Quaxter's behaviour. She was upset because her friend, Charlie Duck, was ill.

About the same time police were called to a house in Darwin following complaints from neighbours that shots were being fired. The front door open, the police warily walked in to find a man lying on a bed with a .22 calibre rifle in his hand. There were numerous holes in the walls and ceiling. The man, when questioned, readily admitted firing the rifle 'I was shooting cockroaches,' he explained. 'It's far more effective than Baygon.'

# DE FACTO PREMIERS
# AND TOMLINSON'S CRUSADE

Political life in the Northern Territory always has had a certain rugged yet breezy informality to it – both inside and outside parliament. It wasn't a phenomenon that emerged in recent years. Back in the 1890s, for example, one of the Northern Territory's first two representatives in the South Australian House of Assembly, Vaiben Louis Solomon[1], was nicknamed 'Black' after winning a bet with a solicitor that he wouldn't streak naked along Darwin's main thoroughfare, Smith Street. Together with a friend, he blackened his body and, posing as an Aborigine and carrying what were described a 'corroborree trimmings' he hot-footed it down the street in his birthday suit. No one recognised him or even gave him a glance, but Solomon collected his winnings. The owner and editor of the *Northern Territory Times* and *Gazette*, Solomon not only became premier of South Australia – for seven days – but went on to become a member of the first Federal Parliament after serving as a member of the fifty-man Constitutional Convention that framed the Federal Constitution.

Eight decades later, in 1977, Paul (Porky) Everingham was elected majority leader of the Northern Territory Legislative Assembly after the surprise defeat of the Country-liberal Party Chief Secretary, Dr Goff (Silver Fox) Letts, by war veteran and former patrol officer, Jack Doolan, in the seat of Victoria River. For Everingham, the days when he indulged in bunfights at the annual dinner of the Northern Territory Law Society were over and until he resigned seven years later to successfully contest the Northern Territory Federal seat – he possibly saw himself as prime ministerial material – Everingham had the reputation as the *enfant terrible* from the Top End. A cow cocky drawl, farmyard candour and pithy comments became his trademarks while his old boss, Dr Letts – the doctorate was a veterinary degree – who went off to become head of the Northern Territory Parks and Wildlife Committee, in a moment of frustration, likened him to a bull in a china shop. (From all accounts the pair didn't particularly like one another). The then Leader of the Opposition, Bob Collins, remarked that the Territory was run 'according to the Gospel of St Paul.' Although his popularity rating before his resignation was eighty per cent (a figure that Labor reluctantly confirmed), it did elicit, from time to time, some tongue-in-cheek letters to the Territory press. Wrote one correspondent: 'His stirring, if slow, speeches would conjure up images of a paradise on earth, the last frontier... a sort of Clayton's Shangri La.' And a piece of graffiti over the hand-drier in Katherine's new public toilets read: 'Press button for election speech from Paul Everingham.' Everingham, too, didn't endear himself to the local press. A long awaited debate between the sitting Labor Member of the House of Representatives, John Reeves (ironically Everingham's old partner in law at Alice Springs) was surreal. The scene was the ABC office in Darwin. Everingham entered, late and unshaven.

First reporter: 'Good afternoon Mr Everingham.'

Everingham: 'Rhubarb to you.'

Second reporter: 'Wouldn't you agree, gentlemen that this election campaign had had about as much snap, crackle and pop as a milk-soaked plate of Corn Flakes?'

Reeves: 'You mean Rice Bubbles?'

Everingham: 'Isn't that some sort of bird?'

And so it went on. Twenty minutes later Everingham, without saying goodbye, stomped out. As a parting shot, the then Independent Member for Nightcliff, Mrs Dawn Lawrie, noting that Everingham could be 'extremely and embarrassingly rude and crude,' advised him that if he wished to do the best for the Territory he should forget trying to score cheap points such as referring to a political opponent as 'the lowest flea on the back of the ALP dog.' But give him his due, as de facto premier Everingham was never reluctant to air his views and, despite the stance of his Canberra colleagues and their leader, was bitterly critical of Indonesia's actions in East Timor, accusing the country, in a speech to the House, of trying to swallow up the Timorese like a big, greedy lizard and that everyone 'just hustles down to the pie cart and has another pie.' He was unorthodox in the Assembly, too, and at times could be seen, half asleep, with his feet propped up on the table during some long-winded speech.

By the time Everingham resigned in 1984 he was regarded by his successor, former soft drink manufacturer and motel owner, Ian Tuxworth, as a political liability for whom there was 'no room at the inn,' to use his rather odd phrase. And Tuxworth believed, rightly or wrongly, that the Northern Territory administration was badly in need of psychological help. So he promptly called up a team of psychologists to 'motivate' his ministry and staff. Cabinet ministers, departmental heads, including their bemused wives, were summonsed to attend a three-day self development course, entitled New Age Thinking, conducted by self-styled American motivator, Louis Tice, founder and chairman of the Seattle-based Pacific Institute. The cost was a hundred and ninety-five dollars per person. It was then revealed that Tuxworth's brother, Bob, was agent for the company, not only in the Territory but also for South Australia. Needless to say, an indignant Tuxworth responded that Bob would certainly not be receiving any direct commission from the company. The course went ahead, but whether it produced any tangible results was a moot point. Meantime, Tuxworth's public relations officers dashed out an effusive press release on the new Chief Minister. The founder of the Crystal Aerated Waters in Tennant Creek was, the release said, a 'slow talking, deliberate man [who] acknowledges with some pride to being just an ordinary boy from the bush.' But, from the dusty playing fields of an isolated mining and pastoral community at Tennant Creek to the plush boardrooms of top level international companies, Ian Tuxworth had displayed the tenacity, diplomacy and level-headed strategy required to be a political leader in one of Australia's fastest growing regions. Laconically remarked Opposition Leader, Bob Collins: 'The best thing about Tuxworth is Ruth Tuxworth,' referring to Tuxworth's wife, a former nurse.

Now it happened that in the late seventies and early eighties, the Country-Liberal Party had a particular thorn in its side, a feisty public servant named John Tomlinson who was employed in the Community Development Department of the Northern Territory Public Service. Tomlinson had distinguished himself by being the first – and only – Australian public servant to be charged with criminal libel for suggesting that a director of a government welfare agency was guilty of murder by failing to supply help to Aboriginal families in need. (The Crown later dropped the charge after Tomlinson apologised). Not only that, but in 1979 the Territory Government attempted to lay charges of sedition against him over the content of some of the courses he taught. Then in 1980, he was charged with five counts arising out of an incident where, in his capacity as secretary of the Northern Territory Council for Civil Liberties, he had called for a full-scale judicial inquiry into the Territory police force and had instanced the police editing of evidence as one of the grounds. The charges were later dropped.

Government members gave a collective sigh of relief when Tomlinson said he wished to resign from the Public Service. In a letter of resignation to the Secretary of the Department, Mr Ray McHenry, Tomlinson said he had come to his decision because he had seen numerous instances of the CLP using public servants for its own, rather than the Territory's interest. 'The CLP's attack on the Aboriginal Land Rights legislation is motivated by short-sighted economic greed,' he said. Aborigines are twenty-five per cent of the citizens of the Territory, yet every time when [they] look as if they might get secure title to any asset which could help them develop towards financial independence, the racist Cabinet, aided and abetted by their legal lackey, conspire to obstruct Aborigines from getting their legal rights.'

Warming to his subject, Tomlinson continued: 'The CLP's snivelling approach towards any multi-national who offers to dig a hole in the territory and leave us the waste would be laughable if the people of the territory weren't the losers. Finally, the decision of the Solicitor-General to charge me with having defamed the ex-director of Child Welfare, who had consistently refused to pay Aborigines the welfare benefits to which they were entitled, has convinced me that there is no place for honest men in the Northern Territory Government.'

Needless to say Tomlinson's resignation was accepted with alacrity. No sooner had be quit than he sat down and wrote a book titled *Betrayed by Democracy*, the front and back covers of which were photographs of him being arrested and manhandled by police. The book was an attack on the Territory Government, the Federal Government, big business, the Rupert Murdoch owned *NT News* ('which could or should change its name to Murdoch's Mouthpiece'), the *Star* newspaper, the ABC, Aboriginal Land Commissioners, including the Honourable Mr Justice Toohey ('he was able to find very good legal reasons why Aborigines should not be given ownership of burial grounds and other sacred sites [and] was able to dredge up complicated legal jargon which also precluded them owning any land of major economic importance') and, last but not least, the Indonesian rape of East Timor with the tacit approval of successive Australian Governments ('Australia [has] given Indonesia two hundred and fifty Land Rovers as part of our military aid; the Timorese are still fighting. Malcolm Fraser, you have openly connived in the murder of the Timorese people.')

Among those in government who disapproved of Tomlinson was Nick Dondas, Deputy Chief Minister and Minister for Health and Sports about whom was written 'there is no doubt that Mr Dondas is regarded affectionately within his party but... there is uncertainty about his intellectual capacity. But he's a quiet achiever with solid grass-root ties to Darwin's ethnic groups.'

It was a hot and humid November day – the wet season was late that year – when trade unionists, lunchtime strollers, public servants, wives and children gathered in a central Darwin park for an anti-budget rally. Among the throng was John Tomlinson. Just before the speeches were about to begin Chief Minister Everingham, Nick Dondas and another Government member, Roger Steele, strolled into view. Spotting the trio, Tomlinson called out: 'Hey, fellows, there come the blokes who have just declared war on full employment.' Dondas responded angrily, shouting 'Get fucked, Tomlinson.'

Two days later, the *Star* newspaper reported the incident: 'Swearing in public, we are forced to admit, is becoming far more acceptable these days than it was in granddad's time and there is no doubt it is part of the rough and ready image of the Territory. But you don't expect to hear prominent people reeling off the more objectionable of expletives in front of women. This week two VERY prominent politicians were in a VERY public place and one rose to a baiting remark by a bystander. The swift rejoinder, consisting of a two-word piece of advice to the baiter, was heard by a number of women – and some of them were not amused.'

A privately circulated newsletter also reported the incident and noted that on the same day, 'Everingham, Chief Minister and Attorney-General, being so impressed with Dondas' wit and repartee, made him Minister for Youth and Recreation.'

But back to Tomlinson[2]. His book probably deserved a greater readership than the patchy reading it received. He was a sincere crusader for Aboriginal land rights and diligently researched the injustices that he felt had been committed.

In 1963, [he wrote] Pastor Doug Nicholls, himself an Aborigine and subsequently Governor of South Australia, cabled the United Nations that in the four year period 1959-1963 more than two million acres of Aboriginal reserve land was alienated to white interests. Buffy Sainte-Marie singing about American Indians' similar experiences summed it up when she said 'It's all in the past people say/but it's still going on here today.' The process of annexing Aboriginal land has continued unabated since Pastor Nicholls' cable. There have been instances such as the armed police party removing Aborigines from their homes, then burning the homes as occurred at Mapoon [in November 1963] as well as far more subtle endeavours such as occurred at Nabarlek in 1978 when the Federal Government in association with the Northern Land Council finally broke sufficient Aboriginal leaders' resistance to allow the mining of uranium in the Arnhem Land Aboriginal Reserve. The Country-Liberal party has set out to destroy Aborigines' ownership of land conferred on them by the Commonwealth. It has done this by refusing to register deeds, a trick it learnt from [Queensland Premier] Bjelke-Petersen's refusal to register Archer River Station bought by the Commonwealth for an Aboriginal group; the threatened revocation of the Gurinji Pastoral Lease; the gazettal of vast tracts of land as town areas so that the

Aboriginal Land Commissioner is excluded from hearing lands claims for such areas; and it has continued to pressure the Commonwealth to water down existing Land Rights legislation. All of which makes a mockery of the declared intention of the Commonwealth to enable Aborigines to hold their tribal land in perpetuity.

# Notes

1. Vaiben Solomon was one of the great characters that indelibly imprinted his personality on the Territory and would be worthy of a book on his own. The son of Judah Moss Solomon, an orthodox Jew who was not only Chief Magistrate, but also Lord Mayor of Adelaide, he was born on May 13, 1853.

Furious at his son's engagement to a young Christian woman, Mary Wigzell, the daughter of a Rundle Street, Adelaide fruiterer, the old man cut him out of his will. Mary later married a Mr Brigland but he died and she was left with an infant son, Harrie. Solomon, then in Darwin, married her and raised the son as his own child.

A laudatory article in the Adelaide press on Solomon's parliamentary performance said few persons had done more to advertise the immense potentialities of 'our northern possession.' 'He never misses an opportunity to discourse upon the richness of the land from every point of view. As a speaker he was most effective, even after allowance is made for the fact that, in his zealous desire to be thorough and to exhaust his subject, he sometimes spoke at great length. He marshalled his facts most carefully and gave expression to them without the slightest hesitancy. He had almost unlimited debating power and could upon occasion be extremely sarcastic. Yet with a confident and easy style and enviable good temper, he delivered his hardest blows with an obvious absence of malice which, after the first impact had been felt, robbed them of any ranking effect. Rarely did he 'carry a heart stain away on his blade.' His knowledge of financial matters stood him in particularly good stead, and he could dissect a Budget with masterly skill and comprehensiveness. He was an ideal stonewaller and whenever the necessity arose kept debates going with greatest dexterity, and apparently tireless energy. Indeed, persistency was one of his strongest characteristics.'

Vaiben Solomon died from cancer of the liver in 1908.

2. At the time of writing, Tomlinson was Dr John Tomlinson, senior lecturer in Social Policy at the Queensland University of Technology.

# FRED FOGARTY AND HIS LAND CLAIM

A Northern Territory Supreme Court judgement by Mr Justice Blackburn early in 1971 appeared to establish, in the words of a Federal Cabinet submission, that 'Aborigines... have no legal rights to land with which they and their ancestors have traditionally been associated.' There was an immediate outpouring of demands for legal change to ensure Aboriginal land rights. Two years later, in September, 1973, the Northern Territory was to witness the first publicised Aboriginal land rights claim, but certainly not in a manner or form that subsequently would occur with other such claims and certainly not one that could possibly have been envisaged by His Honour Justice Blackburn.

The background to the case was fairly straightforward with elements of black humour. For some months prior to September, a part Aboriginal man known as Fred Fogarty, together with several full-blood Aborigines, had camped on land abutting the then Nightcliff Drive-In theatre in Progress Drive, Nightcliff, a leafy northern suburb of Darwin inhabited mainly by well-to-do public servants. Fogarty was a small, nuggetty man with a rolling walk and distinguished himself by habitually wearing a red head-band; he could not by any means be described, as did one young female solicitor who was involved in the subsequent trial, as 'cute.'

Fogarty, along with his small band of followers, sought to occupy an area of land known as Kulaluk as the claimed descendants of the traditional Kulaluk tribe. At the time, however, the area was formally identified as Crown land that had been leased in perpetuity to a white developer, Leo Viscentin, who planned to clear and develop it as a residential subdivision. This also involved reclaiming an area of swamp. Viscentin set to work, employing some workers and hiring earth moving equipment. Fogarty and his followers proceeded to blockade the heavy machinery and, in a confrontation that followed, several trucks and other equipment were firebombed and Viscentin's employees attacked with metal chains and driven off the land.

The incident sparked widespread police and media attention as, for all intents and purposes, it signalled a possible beginning of hostilities between descendants of tribal Aboriginal landowners and white title-holders.

Fogarty subsequently was charged with a number of criminal offences, ranging from assault to causing grievous bodily harm to malicious damage. Oddly, none of his followers, although involved in incitement of Fogarty's actions, were charged with any criminal offence. Following a preliminary committal hearing in the Darwin Magistrate's Court in October, 1973, Fogarty was committed to stand trial before a judge and jury at the next sittings of the Northern Territory Supreme Court. It was as a result of the publicity surrounding Fogarty that the Northern Australian Aboriginal Legal Service decided to engage the services of one of Australia's leading barristers, Francis (Frank) Eugene Galbally, from Melbourne. Galbally had long been associated with representing people in the news and took an immediate interest in representing Fogarty as the circumstances indicated that such actions could well be the forerunner of other land claims. As Galbally was later to point out, the then Minister for Aboriginal Affairs, Gordon Bryant, not long before the Kulaluk incident, had visited the land in question and had told Fogarty and his followers, in the presence of his press entourage, that 'this land is your land' and 'we [the government] are going to give it back to you.' The Minister, Galbally remarked, had unwittingly incited Fogarty to take the law into his own hands.

Galbally arrived in Darwin three days before the trial. Not only was he flamboyant in his court manners, he was as equally colourful in his dress and general demeanour. A towering man in statue, with a booming voice, he conducted his preliminary briefings from his suite in the Travelodge dressed in a Hawaiian shirt and sandals. As a matter of courtesy, however, one of his first tasks was to seek an audience with the trial judge, the Chief Justice, Mr (later Sir) William Foster, who was sometimes viewed as an uncompromising man who relayed little compassion to those appearing before him.

In the meeting in his chambers, the judge forcibly indicated to Galbally that 'this trial has nothing to do with land rights,' but rather the serious issues of 'assaulting workmen with chains.' His Honour made it clear that he would not allow his court to become a 'national showcase' for Aboriginal land claims. Galbally, according to his instructing solicitor, Mr Neil Halfpenny, left the judge's chambers 'seething.' The judge's comments were 'outrageous,' he fumed. It wouldn't happen anywhere else in Australia that a trial judge would so blatantly pre-judge the issue and direct Defence counsel accordingly.

It was at this stage that Galbally was made aware of Fogarty's background and the fact that it did not suggest his ancestry was connected with the traditional land occupiers, the Kulaluk tribe. It appeared that his only identification with Kulaluk arose as a result of his live-in arrangement with one of the Kulaluk women camping on the land. Furthermore, it quickly became apparent to Galbally that Fogarty was a person of limited intellect and was being used to ferment such claims by well-known Darwin white activists.

The opening day of the trial began with the empanelling of the jury, the selection of which was made difficult for Galbally given the absence of prospective jurors with any Aboriginal heritage. Available jurors, from the ranks of Darwin's burgeoning Public Service, were mostly supporters of the Country-Liberal Party which at the time was identified for its anti-Aboriginal land rights stance. But rather than deter him, Galbally saw the empanelling process as an added spur to his general trial approach.

The Crown's case, led by Mr Bill Raby, essentially relied on the evidence of the investigating police and the contractors who were assigned the task of clearing the disputed land. Mr Raby, ponderous, meticulous and fussy, was at great pains to establish that Fogarty was the principal party involved in both the assaults and the fire-bombing. Each of the contractors called had no difficulty in identifying the accused as the person who assaulted them with chains and subsequently set fire to their equipment.

Galbally, on cross-examining the Crown witnesses, sought to unsettle Prosecutor Raby by light-heartedly touching him on the shoulder when referring to earlier examination in chief. It had its desired effect as the jury and the packed courtroom became more engrossed in Mr Raby's growing annoyance at being patted on the shoulder. At one stage several jury members openly chuckled at the prosecutor's futile attempts to avoid being touched. Galbally also sought to confuse the Crown's evidence by suggesting that the identification of Fogarty arose solely out of him being the only part Aboriginal present, rather than a formal facial identification.

As for the police forensic evidence, it was, Galbally suggested, unreliable and vague. The Crown's chief forensic 'expert' had even admitted that he was not only not an expert in firearms, or Molotov cocktails for that matter, but 'not really an expert in anything at all.' However, when Galbally, during cross-examination, referred to the forensic exhibits as 'junk,' Judge Foster decided he had gone too far in demeaning the evidence of police witnesses and curtly told him he would not have the word 'junk' used in his court. Galbally promptly responded: 'With due respect, Your Honour, the word 'junk' is contained in the English dictionary' and with that turned away from the shocked judge and repeated his question to the police witness: 'Now, where did you get this junk from?' From that point onwards the judge did not seek to interfere with Galbally's cross-examination again.

The end of the first day saw the completion of the Crown's case. In terms of Forgarty's defence, Galbally decided to limit the evidence to that of the accused alone. He required Forgarty to support the line of his cross-examination of Crown witnesses by denying that he was the person responsible and that they were mistaken as to identity.

That night, over several bottles of white burgundy, Galbally told his instructing solicitor, Mr Halfpenny, that he needed to brief his client as to his evidence the next day. On the way to Fogarty's caravan on the outskirts of Darwin Galbally became obsessed with the belief that the police were following him and kept telling his driver to check the rear vision mirror. If indeed he was being followed, the police kept well in the background.

It was a surprised Fogarty when Galbally burst into his caravan. Quickly placing eye drops into his blood-shot pupils, Fogarty offered Galbally a drink. Galbally declined and told him in no uncertain terms what his evidence should be the following day. He reminded Fogarty that the Crown case against him was essentially based on identification. It had no admissions or confessions from either him or his followers. It relied, Galbally emphasised, on the identification by the contractors and that identification was based solely on the premise that he was the only part Aborigine on the land on the day in question. All the other Aborigines, the Crown had alleged, were full bloods. Galbally then looked Fogarty in the eye and said:

'Fred, you know that there were other part Aboriginal persons there, don't you?' Before a bewildered Fogarty could reply, Galbally said: 'Fred, you know them – you know who they are. There was Jimmy Ryan, Bill O'Day, Jackie Smith.' At this point Galbally bent forward and, staring Fogarty in the eyes, added: 'Fred, you can say any name you like because no one is going to contradict you. Do you understand?' Fogarty, looking glassy-eyed, nodded, albeit reluctantly. It then occurred to the two lawyers that perhaps their client saw himself as a hero for Aboriginal lands rights, so much so that it was doubtful that he wanted to accede to Galbally's briefing; that perhaps he wanted to be found guilty. There was also another problem: Fogarty was too inarticulate to allow him to make an unsworn statement from the dock.

When the trial resumed, Galbally decided the best course of approach was to offer no formal evidence from the Defence, and to rely solely on his submissions to the jury that the Crown had not proved beyond reasonable doubt that the accused was the person responsible for assault and malicious damage. Notwithstanding his eloquence and showmanship in his final address to the jury, it took them little time in returning a guilty verdict on all charges.

It was after the jury was discharged and the Crown sought to provide some background to the accused that it was revealed that Fogarty was not of Aboriginal descent, but was, in fact, part Maori. Such a revelation possibly vindicated Galbally's decision not to run the defence on Aboriginal land rights issues. One will never know as Galbally's parting comment was: 'You know this whole thing could have been one great hoax by the developer to extract maximum compensation from the Federal Government for a worthless mosquito-infested piece of swamp land. That is to say, he set Fred up as a stooge for Aboriginal land claims.'

Shortly afterwards, the Federal Minister for Aboriginal affairs, Gordon Bryant travelled to the Territory promising to give all the disputed land back to the original tribal inhabitants.

Fred was sentenced to 18 months jail with a non-parole period of nine months. Not long after his release he was found drowned off Kulaluk beach. The Kulaluk land was returned to the remnants of the Kulaluk tribe and the land developer was compensated handsomely by the Federal Government. In April, 1975, Mr Justice Richard Ward was appointed Interim Aboriginal Land Commissioner and the land claims process began. Sadly, Dick Ward, regarded as one of the Territory's greatest men, died two years later.

Nineteen years after the Fogarty case the High Court handed down its historic Mabo decision that recognised the concept of native title. The Court said that native title pre-dated colonisation and had only been extinguished wherever the Crown had granted interest in land to third parties. Native title could no longer be denied or removed for reasons that were unjust.

# HOGAN, THE ANTI-HERO
## AND OTHER EDITORS

It isn't often that journalists get the chance to take the micky out of an unpopular editor. One memorable case occurred in the early sixties when a disgruntled writer on *The Bulletin* who faced the sack penned a cleverly constructed poem that was published, in which the first letter of every line that wasn't indented read, 'Fuck all editors.' John Hogan, a New Zealander who took over as managing editor of the Murdoch-owned *NT News* after Cyclone Tracy, had an unfortunate habit of needlessly ruffling the feathers of quite a number of Territorians. Unlike his predecessor, Jim Bowditch, he just didn't seem to fit in. The London-born Bowditch was a member of the famed Z Force that operated behind Japanese lines during the Second World War. Arriving in the Territory he worked as a stockman, gold miner and axeman before becoming a reporter, then editor of the *Centralian Advocate* at Alice Springs and, later, the *NT News*, finally winning the Walkley Award, journalism's ultimate accolade. He was immensely popular and many stories have been told, and written by Bowditch himself, about his career. Errol Simper who, together with this writer, worked for him during his editorship tells of one occasion that summed up the man when Bowditch was invited to a swish function in Darwin and, on his way to the event, encountered an Aboriginal friend. The Aborigine fell into step with Bowditch and followed him into the function room, only for Bowditch to be told his friend couldn't accompany him because he wasn't wearing shoes. Bowditch promptly raced into the street and managed to catch a startled taxi-driver about to pull away.

Bowditch: 'Cabbie, how much do you want for your shoes?

Cabbie: 'What?'

Bowditch: Your shoes, man. How much do will you take for them?

Cabbie: Mate, are you, er, feeling totally hundred per cent okay?'

The driver eventually left ten dollars richer but barefooted. Bowditch had overcome the dress regulations on behalf of his mate.

Hogan was a different kettle of fish. He remained oddly out of touch with Territorians, his editorials gave unnecessary offence and his action in causing a major criminal trial to be aborted prompted the Chief Justice of the Territory, Sir William Forster, to refer to the *NT News* as 'that wretched paper.' In his first two weeks as editor, he alienated the trade unions by strongly criticising them for continuing their efforts to gain the same post-cyclone benefits that public servants received and also the conservationists for trying to protect the Territory's national parks from mining exploitation. His journalists bore the brunt. One angry politician, Mrs Dawn Lawrie, the highly respected Independent Member for Nightcliff, stung by one of Hogan's editorials, raised the matter in Parliament.

Calling Hogan 'a crazy, stupid, strange and bizarre man' and querying why she had aroused Hogan's ire, Mrs Lawrie launched her attack: 'Mr Speaker, the *NT News*, through its editor who appears to be the arbiter of public morals, public debate and public everything else, has come out yet again this evening in a most peculiar manner. Deciding in my absence that I am a so-called independent, that any further claim of mine to independence would be hypocritical in the extreme and that, as a result of the recent local government elections and the support I received from a variety of people, 'my image as a representative of all is irreversibly tarnished.'

One does wonder, if I am irreversibly tarnished, how indeed I am leading the poll.

Warming to her subject, Mrs Lawrie continued:

> The editorial is slanted in a direction which would have the citizens believe that I am 'a surrogate ALP member; that I am some kind of party hack propped up by the ALP but without formal recognition and that a great mischief has been perpetrated upon the innocent people of Darwin in voting by a majority for me as their lord Mayor. Mr Deputy Speaker, that to me is typical of the peculiar editorials emanating from the present [editor] of the News. We find, in fact, that fate makes strange bedfellows because not only am I regularly castigated in his columns, but the Chief Minister also appears to have incurred his continuing wrath, as has the present Lord Mayor, Cec Black. Now we have all earned his wrath. However, I think it is time the editor of the News opened both his sleepy eyes and got both side of the story so that his present editorials could make a little more sense than they do at present. This one, given the facts, is largely incomprehensible. [It is] a rather nasty, slanted, stupid little editorial.

Hogan was a great proponent of uranium mining. 'Let's stop mucking about and start using the resources we have,' he wrote in another of his editorials. 'Specifically, let's mine, process and sell the Top End's uranium. We have a big barrel of money just waiting for us to start picking it. Now is the time to start.'

For two years he pushed the same line until jaded journalists responded by plastering the reporters' room with anti-uranium stickers. They invariably found them ripped off the following morning. Matters came to a head when Hogan threatened to 'instantly dismiss' (a favourite phrase) anyone he saw sticking up the posters. That evening, he discovered two iridescent stickers on the bumper bar of his company-owned car.

Another well-known Darwin resident whom Hogan antagonised was the flamboyant Sandra Holmes, mentor of the great Aboriginal artist, Yirawala, and a feeling of antipathy was apparently mutual. It was in reference to this feud that a couple of senior journalists, including Matt Handbury, Murdoch's nephew who was chief of staff, wrote a story which they substituted for the page one lead, stopping the presses during the afternoon run to make the switch. At the time Hogan was away in Sydney and his deputy, Alec Martin was in hospital. Headed 'Editor Flees Voodoo Curse' in huge type with a sub-head 'Deputy Struck Down,' the article read:

> The editor of the *NT News*, Mr John Hogan, has fled Darwin under a voodoo curse from a local sorceress. But his deputy, assistant editor, Mr Alec Martin, who flaunted the threats, has been struck down by a mysterious ailment and is in an unknown condition in Darwin Hospital. The sorceress, in flowing robes and with her death black hair piled high in a pyramid of doom, issued her grave warning in the *NT News* office recently. She scattered bark, snake's skin and garlic cloves in the foyer. Mr Hogan refused to leave the security of his office and even the bold Mr Martin shrunk from facing the hateful wrath of witches tidings (sic). Antagonised all the more by their failure to stand up to her, her voice rose to a thin wail as the girls at the front counter froze in terror. Rumours that she stuck 15cm needles through an effigy of Mr Hogan were unfounded. But Mr Hogan is understood to have developed an uncontrollable aversion to his wife's after-dinner habit of doing her sewing before the television. He is in Sydney seeking

advice on how to save himself from this predicament. Meanwhile, Mr Martin lies in Darwin hospital muttering inarticulate streams of words questioning how he, once again, was the one to take the brunt of the situation. His medical attendants are unable to find any cause of his ailment beyond the unspeakable...voodoo or black magic. The feud between Mr Hogan and the sorceress is long-standing, dating from the day, soon after his arrival in Darwin, when she burst into his office...

The rest of the story is, unfortunately, obliterated.

A number of copies were printed before the presses were stopped again and the story replaced by the original lead. Needless to say, they were quickly snaffled up. Whether Hogan was told about it is unknown, but nothing was ever said and no one was threatened with 'instant dismissal.'

Hogan was one of numerous editors this writer has worked under. One, an Englishman, Sid Bolstridge who was a keen race-goer, decided to impart his knowledge of the sport of kings by penning a weekly tipping column called 'From Paddock to Punter'. Some eighteen months later it was pointed out to him that he'd never actually picked a winner. It was the end of his role as a tipster. Then there was Frank Puddicombe who suffered a fatal heart attack in the composing room. More than thirty years after his death, a friend, one of the compositors at the time, was staying with me and we were remembering fellow employees in those distant days. My friend, who had migrated from Holland, suddenly said, 'I killed Frank Puddicombe.' I looked at him in astonishment and before I could reply, went on: 'I made a mistake and transposed the introduction with the second paragraph in his lead story. He was furious, went red in the face. 'You fucking Dutch bastard,' he said, and clutched his chest and died on the floor of the composing room.'

There were a few editors who fancied themselves as gurus, but only one in the history of Australian newspapers became a professional guru. Barry Long, for whom this writer worked as a young journalist back in the late 1950s, was editor of the Sydney *Sunday Mirror*. He quit the game in 1963 and went off to look for the meaning of life, first to India and then to England. Returning to Australia twenty years later, he became the foremost Australian born and bred spiritual guru. He died in December, 2003, aged seventy-seven, and his obituarist wrote:

> He was the author of a series of books, including best sellers on how to meditate and how to practise a spiritual life and his work is translated into eleven languages. His *Origins of Man and the Universe* is described as a prophetic account of cosmic mysteries telling how both science and religion got it wrong about the Big Bang.

There was one editor who is remembered with unusual fondness, Jack Finch, or Finchy as he was called, who was editor of the Sydney *Truth* (and later chief of staff of the *Daily Mirror*) when it was owned by the 'Almighty' and irascible Ezra Norton, before the days of Rupert Murdoch. Finchy was a ruddy faced, rotund little man who had two favourite sayings: 'Jazz it up, son, jazz it up' and 'She's apples.'

One Saturday night Finchy had his usual call from Ezra.

'Have you done this?' Ezra asked.

'Yes, she's apples, Mr Norton,' Finchy replied.

'And what about that?'

'She's apples, Mr Norton.'

'And I hope there won't be any more bloody libels… I'm sick of them.'

'She's apples, Mr Norton.'

A brief pause, and then it came: 'Right, Finch… now that's attended to, get a crate of them and ram them up your arse.'

# THE SAGA OF NEMARLUK
# THE GREAT FOLK HERO

*Spirits dwell in darkness deep*
*Firelight flickers;*
*Glistening bodies sleep*
*White man came –*
*Primitive bonds,*
*Tribal songs,*
*Lost forever,*
*Spirits weep.*
*– John Reed*

The saga of Nemarluk is one of the great dramas of the Northern Territory. It is rich in characters and incidents, the protagonists being a tribal leader many believed to be a 'superman' and a prejudicial judge.

His Honour, Mr Justice Thomas Alexander (Tommy) Wells, arrived in Darwin in 1933, taking over from the Acting Judge, W H Sharwood. No sooner had he settled in than he began making his sentiments about Aborigines known. In the Supreme Court he twice advocated flogging of Aborigines convicted of assault. In sentencing Roy Antdoolaway, the judge lamented that the 'boy' (he was twenty-five years old) had to be sent to jail because the law did not allow flogging. Aborigines, he said, were 'getting out of hand' and 'becoming cheekier,' all as a direct and inevitable result of government policy. 'Do-gooders' who intervened in a case involving an alleged assault of Aborigines by a policeman were scathingly criticised from the Bench. The word 'Aboriginal', he once remarked during a hearing for the custody of a part Aboriginal child, was concocted by someone with a 'liking for high-sounding words but it had no meaning.' His refusal to accept evidence given by Aborigines, wrote Peter Elder in the *Northern Territory Dictionary of Biography* was seen when he sentenced Charles Priest to nine months' gaol for criminal libel. 'Priest had published a pamphlet accusing Constable (Fred) Don of seducing an Aboriginal house-maid. The judge dismissed the evidence of the Aborigines as untrue and so protected the policeman's reputation.' In another case, Elder wrote, Wells' Associate, the twenty-two-year-old Eileen O'Neil, was badgered in court by a solicitor when she was the Acting Registrar in Bankruptcy. 'She put her plight to the judge, who promptly denied the solicitor the right to appear in the court.' The judge also urged that the proposed expenditure of forty thousand pounds on a new Aboriginal compound should be drawn to the attention of the Parliamentary Works Committee as a scandalous waste of money and the worst thing that could be done for them. The proposed compound would attract more Aborigines to the town where they would inevitably get into trouble. Of a proposal that twenty separate 'shacks' should be built for Aboriginal couples, His Honour said that this was 'far too elaborate.'

Self opinionated, eccentric and stubborn, he often clashed with the Native Affairs Branch, prompting its director, Mr F H Moy, to express his 'strong resentment' at the judge's 'vitriolic remarks' about the branch from the Bench.

Born in February, 1888, near Wagga Wagga in NSW, Wells was the son of a farmer and grazier, Ezekiel, and his wife Rose Ann. Tall, well built and physically strong, he exhibited considerable talent as a boxer when a young man. Before enlisting in the Australian Imperial Force (AIF) in 1917, he worked as a court reporter at the NSW Supreme Court. Wounded in France and suffering from the effects of mustard gas, he was finally discharged as a corporal in 1919 when he resumed his career as a court reporter. Studying in his spare time, he completed his law degree at

Sydney University and was admitted to the NSW Bar in 1924. Nine years later, at the age of forty-five, he was appointed to the Bench of the Northern Territory Supreme Court.

It was this judge, then, who presided over a murder trial in 1934 that, at the time, aroused considerable interest in the southern newspapers all of which had the accused man, Nemarluk, convicted even before he was found guilty. Chief of the Cahn-mah and undisputed leader of his so-called Red Band of close followers, whose tribal lands comprised an area around the Fitzmaurice River south-west of Darwin and near the border of Western Australia, Nemarluk, after escaping from custody and eluding police for six months, was sentenced to death for the murder of a Japanese pearler, although the sentence was later commuted to life imprisonment.

More than sixty years have passed since Nemarluk, in all probability suffering from TB, died in Darwin's Fannie Bay Jail. Representations were made for him to be repatriated to his own country but were ignored by the authorities. During his prime, superlatives were lavished on him: he was an Aboriginal superman, a superb athlete and bushman who consistently evaded capture by travelling for long distances carefully placing each foot under, instead of on top of, grass tuffs or, while in stony country, picking his way cautiously from one patch of firm ground to another making sure that no pebbles were displaced, in order to hide his tracks. In his book, *Nemarluk*, an imaginative account based on fact, of Nemarluk's time on the run from police, the prolific Australian author, Ion (Jack) Idriess, called him the 'King of the Wilds,' and 'one of the last of the Stone Age men'. Wrote the Darwin correspondent of the Melbourne *Herald* in 1933: 'As Nemarluk is 6ft 2in in height, and is a superman among Aborigines in strength and endurance, the searchers believe that he will run almost continuously for two days and nights.' The same correspondent, two days earlier, also wrote: 'If he succeeds [in reaching his tribal lands] it is feared that he would become a serious menace to any police sent after him. Further, he might unsettle his countrymen. He would be the greatest hero in their folk history and as such would be capable of exerting great power over the already dangerous and recalcitrant tribesmen in that vast territory between the Victoria and Daly Rivers. The situation... is grave.'

But was Nemarluk guilty of the crime with which he was charged? Long after Nemarluk's death one of Australia's leading criminal lawyers, Frank Gallbally, researched the case and came to the conclusion that there had been a miscarriage of justice. That had he been brought before a criminal court today he could not have been convicted. Whatever the case, the prosecution's evidence was based on circumstantial evidence and the doubtful testimony of Nemarluk's wives.

The area where Nemarluk was born was known as the Wild lands.

> Towards the west, [Idriess wrote] it is bounded by the Daly River, to the south by the Victoria. Its north and northwest is the wild coast. Far inland it is hemmed in by a maze of ranges that are a labyrinth of canyons and gorges and walls of cliffs protecting inaccessible hideouts. Fronting the ranges are the foothills. And then the plain country; the Moyle River country with its miles upon miles of swamps. Running from the mountains through the plain country nearly midway to the south, to empty eventually near the mouth of the Victoria River runs the Fitzmaurice River, probably the gloomiest, loneliest, most dangerous river in Australia.

Nemarluk grew up in an era when the bonds of tribal discipline were being weakened by white invasion of old hunting grounds. Clashes between Aborigines and Japanese pearlers and shark fishers also were frequent, the Japanese persistently flouting a ban on them entering tribal reserves and kidnapping Aboriginal women. Nemarluk and his Red Band saw it as an obligation and duty to protect their people and their lands from the invaders. However, it wasn't until he was thirty-two years of age when the events occurred that led to arrest and dramatic escape from custody and his ultimate trial before Justice Wells.

In July 1931, according to police, the shark fishing lugger *Ouida* allegedly sailed into Treachery Bay near the mouth of the Fitzmaurice River Bay in what is now the Daly River Port Keats Aboriginal Land. Aboard were Captain Yoshikiya Nagata, and two other Japanese, Yusama Owashi, forty-four, and Ryukichi Yoshida, thirty-nine. There was also a small crew of Aborigines from Melville Island. They allegedly were greeted by Nemarluk and made welcome, the visitors suppling liquor and tobacco and Nemarluk supplying women. They remained on board until Nagata, feeling he was safe, went ashore where he was promptly shot. Yoshida and Owashi, still on board, allegedly were attacked with tomahawks and had their heads split open. It was claimed their bodies were then thrown into the sea but were never found.

However, on August 18, 1931, shortly after the alleged murders, Patrick Dennis Connors, master pearler and Northern Territory manager for Victor Clark, owner of the *Ouida*, made a statutory declaration, declared at Darwin, stating that the lugger was reported lost at sea on or about July 21, 1931 that that the three Japanese crewmen, Nagata, Owashi and Yoshida were drowned. Connors continued: 'As soon as practicable after receipt of report, I caused a search to be made by one of my employees namely James

Gonzales at sea and on the coast adjacent to scene of reported wreck but I am now informed by the said Gonzales and verily believe that no trace was found of the [Japanese]. I verily believe that Nagata, Owashi and Yoshida were drowned at sea as a result of the *Ouida* being capsized.'

Connor's statutory declaration was corroborated by Mr D Miner, head keeper of Point Charles Lighthouse who, in a letter to Mr A Weller, acting sub-collector of Customs, Darwin, dated July 24, 1931, said he had been told by Mr Mitchelmore that two natives had arrived at his station the previous day and that a lugger owned by Mr Clark had 'turned over' in the vicinity of Perin (sic) Island and that three Japanese drowned. 'The native boys,' wrote Mr Miner, 'getting clear managed to pick up the lugger's dinghy and made their way up to Point Charles. I am sending this report over by native Paddy and am also sending with him the natives that were at the scene of the accident for your inspection as you may get more information out of them than they gave me.'

The following day Sergeant R Bridgland, of Darwin, in a letter to his inspector, said that three Melville Island Aborigines had arrived from Point Charles in a canoe and had reported the loss of a lugger and three Japanese fishermen. Taking charge of the trio, he brought them to Darwin police station.

> Aboriginal Bobby, who speaks fairly good English, informed me that the Japanese were shark fishing in the vicinity of Melville Island the moon before this one and had given them a job on the lugger and after leaving Melville Island they had cruised so far as Port Essington and then returned to Shoal Bay and afterwards sailed down around Point Charles towards Perron Island group. It appears that just after hauling the anchor and cruising along with a full sail to a head wind with one of the Japanese at

the tiller, and the other two Japanese down below in their bunks the lugger shipped a big sea and the Aboriginals undid the rope which was lashed around the dinghy and as the lugger sank the dinghy floated off and the three Aboriginals viz Billy, Bobby and a boy about nine years swam out and got into the dinghy and after rowing around the coast for five days arrived at Point Charles and reported same to the Head keeper.

Sgt Bridgland concluded: 'From enquiries made from the Aboriginals I have not the slightest doubt that there are not any suspicious circumstances in connection with the disaster. The boat as far as we can ascertain belonged to V J Clark and is named *Ouida*.'

However, Mounted Constable Ronald Pryor later cast some doubt on Sgt Bridgland's report. A week or so after the *Ouida* was reported missing he conducted a 'very keen' search around the Perron Islands and although no wreckage or men were found, he was not satisfied with the result 'or that the lugger is lost as the abos (sic) have stated,' he wrote in a report to his senior officer, Superintendent A V Stretton. Two months went by and then, on October 6, the Government Resident of North Australia, Lieutenant-Colonel Robert Hunter Weddell, who had little sympathy for Aborigines, sent a coded telegram to the Department of Home Affairs in Canberra. Decoded and marked 'for Minister's information' it read:

Ship *Maroioia* arrived from Victoria River 5th October and reported lugger answering the description *Ouida* on the beach near Port Keats. Report from police Daly River states Aboriginal Smiler had in his possession rifle alleged obtained by him from Aboriginals near Fitzmaurice River who reported four white men presumably Japanese murdered by

Aboriginals. Lugger beached and ransacked. Having no boat I am sending police party investigate and hiring above mentioned ship costing 14 pounds per diem for the five days. Fitzmaurice tribe in possession of firearms and extremely hostile and have stated intention to shoot any police party.

His coded telegram, he said in a follow up letter to the department, was proof that the *Ouida* was not lost but apparently beached by Aborigines after murdering the Japanese crew. A statement based on Weddell's wire was released to the Press, the *Sydney Morning Herald* headlining the story with 'JAPANESE, Murder by Aborigines ON PEARLING LUGGER.' Nemarluk and his Red Band already were convicted.

The following day, October 7, Mounted Constable Albert Koop, who later was to prosecute Nemarluk, together with Mounted Constable John Mahony and two trackers, Sambo and Bul Bul (about whom we'll hear more of later) left Darwin on the *MV Maroubra* to search for the missing lugger and her crew. In a report to Superintendent Stretton written a week later, Constable Koop said the lugger was found at a point about two hundred miles from Darwin on the western coast between Point Hay and Port Keats. It was high on the beach and had an anchor at the stern and the bow 'proving that she had been deliberately placed on the beach.'

An examination of the lugger showed that all personal effects belonging to the crew and all removable fittings had been taken and bloodstains on the platform at the stern of the boat pointed to foul play. An attempt had been made to scrape these bloodstains off,' Constable Koop wrote. His report continued: 'An immediate search was commenced on the beach and foreshore for the bodies of the crew and this search was continued for three days. Tracks round the lugger and signs round camps on the foreshore showed that abo's (sic) had been there on the day we arrived and there was evidence of a hurried evacuation. Two sails and other ship's gear were found in the vicinity of the abo's camps and some of the personal belongings of the crew were discovered hidden near the camps. The number of camps around showed that large number of abo's had been in the neighbourhood for some considerable time. Tracks were followed into the mangrove swamps about two miles distant and a hidden camp was discovered there. This camp, in the opinion of the trackers, was made by the abo's responsible for the tragedy and they consider that the murderers hid there for some days after the offences were committed. A shovel spear was found in this camp and this may be useful later on for purposes of identification. At another camp was seen where two flies had been stretched and there is no doubt that these flies were made from the missing sail off the lugger.

Constable Koop said an area of about fifty square miles was searched to find further evidence, but nothing was located. Sand banks were probed but again nothing was found. He stated that many temporary lagoons would be under water following the wet season and speculated that it was possible that one of these was the scene of the alleged shooting of Nagata.

The foreshore, for about six miles to the south and as far as Point Hay to the north was patrolled and various articles from the lugger found, but no trace of any bodies could be obtained. I nought back various personal belongings which have been identified as being the property of the missing crew, also a bloodstained nullah nullah found concealed near the lugger, which may have been used in the alleged killing on the boat. I consider it certain that the crew have been wiped out by Aboriginals. The abo tribes in this vicinity are noted for their treacherous and murdering proclivities and it will be remembered that in 1905 a boat from Bradshaws with a crew of five was attacked and the whole party massacred by Aboriginals not far from the scene of the present tragedy. The myall abo's (sic) are reinforced by semi civilised natives from cattle stations who bring with them the knowledge of the use of firearms and it is probable that the firearm looted from the lugger will be used against the police when they attempt to arrest the perpetrators of this alleged crime. I am of the opinion that s strong party, operating on both land and sea, should be sent as early as possible to endeavour to bring the offenders to trial and that they must be prepared for active resistance from the abo's concerned when they are located. I believe if the Melville Island abo's who formed the rest of the crew of the lugger are located that the evidence they can give will result in the identification and conviction of the offenders providing, of course, that we are successful in apprehending them. During the whole of our stay down the coast we were aware that Aboriginals were in the vicinity but all our attempted to get contact with them proved abortive. We frequently followed fresh tracks for miles without being able to overtake the abo's, the country is heavily timbered and affords excellent cover.

Constable Koop concluded: 'The lugger was floated off the beach by J Hayles, master of the *Maroubra*, and towed into Darwin.'

Constable Koop continued his investigations and at the end of November, 1931, submitted a second report to Superintendent Stretton.

Two of the Melville island boys who accompanied the ill-fated crew of the *Ouida* on her last trip down the western coast were brought to Darwin on the 27th inst by the Mission schooner, *St Francis*. The third boy is still on Melville Island, but Father Gsell of the Mission forwarded a statement, said to be taken from the boy, regarding the matter. I have fully questioned the elder of the boys, now in Darwin, and from his replies and the statement furnished by Father Gsell I have elicited the following information. The lugger *Ouida* was sailing down the western coast and when between Cape Hay and Port Keats fires were seen ashore. The Japanese immediately put in despite the fact that the Melville Island boys warned them that the natives there were cheeky. Natives from the shore immediately came aboard and were given food and tobacco. The next morning the Japanese asked for lubras and these were brought out to the boat and remained aboard that night. The next day the Tender were ashore to shoot ducks, taking the dinghy and accompanied by the Melville Island boy named Bob. Some time later seven abo's (sic) came out to the lugger in a canoe bringing a few ducks. They were asked where the Tender was and replied that he was shooting kangaroos for the abo's ashore. Three shots had been heard previously. After awhile the Melville Island boys left on board became uneasy owing to the protracted absence of the tender and the actions of the seven natives on board and they decided to take the canoe and go ashore to look for the Tender. They had noticed that when the seven abo's came aboard they bought a tomahawk and when they were some distance from the lugger the younger of the two looked back and saw that the abo's were in the act of killing the Japanese aboard with the tomahawk. He immediately told the other boy who looked and saw what was being done and them rowed as hard as he could towards the shore calling out to their mate who was minding the dinghy and telling him what had happened. The man ashore came out with the dinghy and they all got in and pulled for their lives. The abo's on board called to them to return and then gave chase with the lugger but could not sail in the shallow water where the dinghy was kept and so abandoned the chase. After nine sleeps the Melville Island boys reached Point Charles and came on the Darwin.

Mounted Constable Koop said the Melville Islanders changed their story after being interrogated by police and that the reason they told a false tale was that they were too frightened to tell the truth, fearing that they might be suspected of being implicated. 'I am now satisfied that the story they now tell is substantially correct and that the boys now here will be valuable witnesses when the offenders are apprehended as they can identify the seven who did the murders on the lugger.'

As soon as weather conditions permitted – the country at that time was impassable due to the west season – a police party set out to arrest the alleged killers. But it wasn't until almost a year later that five men, Minemarra, Montespare (otherwise known as (Mangul Mangul),

Nargoon, Marragin and Mankee, all members of Nemarluk's Red Band, were rounded up and charged with the murder of Nagata and committed for trial at the criminal sessions of the Supreme Court on November 2, 1932. The case, before acting Judge Sharwood who was sent from Canberra to conduct the case, was painfully slow, observed the *Canberra Times* 'owing to the inability of the accused to understand a single word of English.'

*The Age* newspaper ran the story in more detail: 'When the case opened the defending counsel (Mr Foster) offered a plea of guilty to manslaughter, but the judge ruled that such a plea could not be accepted in a murder case, so the plea of not guilty was entered. Mr Foster applied for a ruling that the prisoners, being savages, were incapable of understanding the nature of the charge or the proceedings taken against them, and that they were therefore not guilty through incompetence. The judge ruled, however, that he was unable to make a departure from the usual custom. No evidence was called for the defence, but in reply to Mr Foster, a key Crown witness, a lubra named Eyel, after being asked a number of questions, said she would say 'yes' to anything counsel for the accused asked. 'Mr Foster promptly sat down,' noted the *Northern Standard's* reporter.

The judge, the *Age* report continued, 'summed up strongly against the defendants, stating there was strong evidence of the killing of Nagata and that [the] defendants had aided and abetted the crime. The judge added he was sorry Nemarluk was not in the dock also. There was no evidence to warrant a verdict of manslaughter. Accused had deliberately agreed to murder the Japanese. There was no evidence of a quarrel over the lubras. The jury deliberated for twenty minutes and returned with a verdict of murder. The judge then pronounced sentence of death. A second series of charges against the five for the murder of the two other Japanese was not proceeded with.'

The report concluded by remarking that the original story of what occurred – that the *Ouida* had sunk in a storm and the Japanese had drowned – was not investigated in court and no mention was made of it by counsel for the defence.

Three weeks before the five men were to be hanged, the matter was raised in Federal Parliament by Mr George Lawson. A report in Hansard said Mr Lawson addressed the Minister for the Interior (Mr J A Perkins): 'Having received numerous letters of protest from private individuals and public bodies relative to the death sentences… I ask the Minister whether in view of the primitive nature and tribal customs of the natives he will use his influence to have their sentences commuted to a term of imprisonment?'     Six days later the Governor General signed a Warrant to Sheriff commuting the sentences to life imprisonment 'without the benefit of the regulations relating to remissions for good conduct.'

The search now turned to their tribal chief and alleged ringleader, Nemarluk, but in the meantime Judge Sharwood's ruling that he 'could not make a departure from the usual custom' was taken up by Helen Baillie, honorary secretary of the Aboriginal Fellowship Group. 'Does not this show the need of special courts for trying Aboriginal and 'mixed' cases with a judge who has a knowledge of anthropology and so is able to ensure justice for the native?' she asked in a strongly worded letter to the Minister for the Interior.

According to Dr Elkin, an expert on anthropology, native laws and customs are very complicated. A native has no knowledge of white law and it is obviously unjust to try him by a law he does not understand. If you read Dr Elkin's little book, `Understanding the Aboriginal' you will see that according to native law when a man takes a lubra he becomes a member of the tribe and must give presents of tobacco etc and most of the troubles with the blacks occur because the whites do not know this law so do not keep it. This is what happened in this case. The Japanese were breaking Aboriginal law not because they took the women, but because when the action made them members of the tribe they did not carry out their obligations to give presents. No mention is made of the fact that the Japanese had broken white law in taking the women.

Ms Baillie stressed the fact that in accordance with Government policy for Aborigines there were a number of strict regulations, including one that stated that any person other than an Aborigine or 'half-caste' who unlawfully had carnal knowledge of an Aborigine or 'half-caste' was guilty of an offence, the penalty being one hundred pounds fine or three months jail or both. The regulations also stipulated that no female Aborigine was to be employed on or about any ship or boat. Mr Perkins responded by saying that the question of the establishment of a special court for the trial of Aborigines had been engaging the attention of the Government for some time. Various suggestions and schemes had been investigated but no satisfactory solution to the problem had been found. Whenever an Aborigine was brought before a court, he was represented by a Protector and, where possible, 'by the best legal counsel procurable.' It would seem,' he went on, 'that the most practicable and suitable way of dealing with this matter is to provide that the judge of a court, when dealing with cases in which Aborigines are concerned shall give due regard to native customs.'

The following month Nemarluk finally was caught while asleep in a mangrove swamp. Chained to a stirrup iron he was eventually brought to Darwin from Victoria River on the *MV Maroubra* and appeared in the Magistrate's Court before special magistrate, Mr Victor Lampe, charged with Owashi's murder. 'He had evaded arrest so often, it was said, that he would not be taken without shooting, which the police were forbidden to do,' reported the *Sydney Morning Herald*. Nemarluk later revealed that during his time on the run he had to dive into the crocodile-infested Fitzmaurice River to throw his pursuers off the scent. Straddling a floating log he was swept downstream afraid to put ashore while police followed. After dark he could just make out the dark snouts of crocodiles keeping pace with the drifting log. One by one his stock of spears melted away as he jabbed desperately at them. Finally, in the middle of the night he came ashore, climbed into a tree and lashed himself to a branch with strong vines and managed to get some sleep. Next morning he jumped to the ground between three crocodiles that had spent the night the base of the tree, and sped to safety.

The Crown witnesses at the committal hearing were Nemarluk's two wives, Marpoo (or Marboo) and Nunnunnie but both were referred to as Nellie. Through an interpreter named Bangtail, the women told the court that when *Ouida* anchored, a number of Aborigines went alongside in their native craft asking for tobacco, which was refused. They then talked about killing the Japanese, but deemed it politic to send their lubras over first, and then demand tobacco. Again they were refused. Captain Nagata was then told that there were plenty of ducks ashore and, arming himself with a shotgun, set out on a shooting expedition. He did not return. Carrying ducks, the Aborigines then went aboard and asked the lubras, who had remained on the boat, for tobacco, but they replied they still had not received any. Two days later, the women claimed they overheard Nemarluk and another Aborigine, Minemarra, talking about killing the two remaining Japanese on board and 'getting level.' Shortly afterwards, the Japanese were attacked by tomahawks 'on the neck' and killed and their bodies thrown into the sea. The two Melville Island crew were in a dinghy when the alleged murders were committed. They hoisted sail and 'cleared away.' Nemarluk and Minemarra, on board the lugger, gave chase, intending to kill the Melville Islanders but, being unable to catch them, returned to the original anchorage and stripped the boat of its portable items.

Commented the Melbourne *Herald's* correspondent on May 8: 'In striking contrast to the grimly dramatic nature of the lubras' allegations was the cheery way in which they recited them. Curious, too, sounded the formal submission by the police prosecutor, Constable Koop, to the restriction against a wife giving evidence against her husband did not apply in this case.'

Special magistrate Lampe found that Nemarluk had a case to answer and committed him for trial in the Supreme Court on September 28, 1933. He was remanded in custody and taken to Fannie Bay Jail where he joined eight other Aborigines, including Tiger, his tribal brother and member of the Red Band who, only a few months before, had been sentenced to life imprisonment for the murder of two European prospectors, Kock and Arinski on Mudgejack Creek, a tributary of the Fitzmaurice. Led by Tiger, the small band of Aborigines had followed the prospectors until they settled down for the night and then speared them. The bodies were cut up into fragments and buried on the river bank.

As the date of his trial neared, Nemarluk made a daring escape. Early one morning, together with four other Aborigines serving life sentences for murder, he marched through the back gate on a routine job of carrying sanitary buckets from the jail to dump into the sea, two hundred metres away. They were in charge of a guard armed with a revolver. As they halted momentarily while the warder shut the gate, Nemarluk dropped his cans and sprinted, 'at great speed' according to the guard, for the corner of the jail fence about sixty metres away.

The Melbourne *Herald* ran the story:

The warder had only time to draw his revolver and fire one shot [he missed] before Nemarluk hurdled the wire fence enclosing the superintendent's garden and, turning to the left, put the fence between him and the warder. He raced across the garden, took another five feet fence in his stride, then sprinted across a road and in a few seconds was lost to view in the jungle of 6ft high grass, interlaced with mangroves, banyans, bamboos, lawyer vines and luxuriant undergrowth. Fearing that the others might bolt the warder raised the alarm and herded the remainder of the working fatigue back behind the jail fence before giving chase. He was joined in a minute by other warders and the alarm given to police in the town brought trackers and police to the spot in a few minutes. The search party followed the fugitive's path where he had crashed through he undergrowth for about 400 yards then lost all trace of him. Splitting up and sending back word for reinforcements the searchers then began the hopeless task of beating the jungle. The vegetation is so thick and vision is limited to five yards, and the police would almost have to step on the fugitive before they could see him. Wardens, with trusted Aboriginal prisoners, were sent to join the party and plans are being made for further reinforcements from the town. Searchers believe that their chances of capturing the fugitive who defied police attempts to arrest him for more than two years after the Port Keats killing are very remote.

Meantime, the hapless jail guard, Mr Leonard Samut, despite his protestations that he, at all times, carried out his duties at the jail 'in a zealous and loyal manner,' was reprimanded for his carelessness, fined one pound and warned that a repetition of the offence would result in his dismissal.

The hunt for Nemarluk was sensationalised by southern newspapers. Again presupposing his guilt, sub editors seemed to vie with one another for the most lurid and defamatory headline. 'Abo Killer in Territory' declared the Sydney *Sun*, 'Fugitive Black' stated the *Canberra Times*, 'Tracker and Murderer' asserted the Melbourne *Herald* on October 17 while the next day it announced, 'Black Killer Still Free.' Reports were peppered with words such as 'black desperado,' 'ferocious,' 'uncivilised,' 'runaway savage,' 'giant murderer,' 'masterly cunning,' 'wily', 'Aboriginal treachery' and 'cheeky feller.' Echoing the Melbourne *Herald*, the Sydney *Sunday Sun* of October 28 also noted the extent of Nemarluk's influence – a power that certainly concerned the police and worried the missionaries: 'Swift pursuit has commenced. It is realised that if Nemarluk gets back to his own country and regains his strength he will become a great hero among the blacks. In that event every white man venturing into Nemarluk's territory will carry his life in his hands.' However, the *Northern Standard's* columnist, 'Pegasus,' took a much lighter view of Nemarluk's escape. Under the heading 'Banny Bay Races' he wrote:

> Recently the officials of Bob's Home for Bad Boys, one of the show places for visitors to Darwin, held an impromptu race meeting. The first race, I have to tell you of is the Banny Bay Flutter details of which are as follows: Banny Bay Flutter. 1st prize Freedom – Lotoluk, a powerfully built black with plenty of bone and sinew, who was being prepared at the stables of Wob Balker for trial in Darwin, decided to enter for the above event, unbeknown to his trainer. The race took place on September 23. Lotoluk

getting a good start beat the rifle by about 100 yards, Sam Lemut being very slow on the pistol finger which tardiness cost him one off his role. When the report sounded somewhere behind him, Lucky sprinted, showing how careful handling and regular feeding had improved his pace. Taking the fences in his stride he strode into the jungle, and on glancing over his shoulder, gave his rivals the 'raspberry.' He then slackened to a walk, for well the big black knew he must conserve his strength. Once the gun went off and 'Wob' had announced to the 'head' that the race was open to all comers, a great number of starters took the field, including some of the slickest coppers, shod with gas wagons. Lotoluk, however, was never seriously troubled for 23 days and was quietly resting in the country around Delissaville when Fredon and his Man Friday, accompanied by some other dusky aspirants for Lucky's crown, challenged his right to the lead. Lotoluk, who was still somewhat unbroken, grabbed the bit in his teeth so to speak and after a short, sharp and sudden tussle, made off. Again he beat the gun by yards but found the black boy much quicker on the draw. Lucky was clear and still missing when his challengers last glimpsed him; still, hopes were entertained that he had been hit and that he would be unable to hold the lead. His pursuers were doomed to disappointment and it is believed Lotoluk will go the distance. Some of his competitors were poor sprinters for, after taking his dust for a short distance they `skied the wipe' and when the last bulletin reached (this) writer Lotoluk still held a commanding lead. Late information is to the effect that the Bouncing Boy, after his win over Joe, is to enter for the Banny Bay Flutter. The positions are: Lotoluk... 1; Smile... 2; Fredon... 3.

The reference by Pegasus to the challenge to Lotoluk by Fredon, his Man Friday and 'other dusky aspirants' referred to the famous fight between Nemarluk and the Aboriginal tracker, Smile (not 'Smiler' as he was named in the southern press, confusing the police tracker with another 'notorious' alleged Aboriginal murderer).

Nemarluk had been on the run for two months when, acting on a tip off, Constable Fred Don, accompanied by Smile and three other Aborigines, went across Darwin Harbour to Delissaville, an old time sugar plantation, and raided an Aboriginal camp. A colourful account of what happened was published in the Melbourne *Herald* of October 17, 1933:

> One of the most thrilling hand-to-hand encounters in the history of the Northern Territory police force took place at dawn today when a police party attempted to capture the notorious native murderer, Nemarluk. Hero of the fight was the black tracker, Smiler. Nemarluk was captured in a camp at Delissaville Island, across the border from Darwin. Creeping up on Nemarluk just as dawn broke and taking him by surprise, Smiler fought a life and death struggle with him for more than a quarter of an hour before the desperate escapee was eventually thrown over a [50ft] cliff, leaving Smiler too exhausted to move and another police tracker unconscious on the ground, felled by a blow from a 10lb lump of ironstone. Spears, waddies, bullets and revolvers played their part in the grim encounter. The fate of Nemarluk is unknown, but it is believed that he is lying near the spot of the encounter badly wounded from a bullet fired by Smiler. Police are still combing the island for him. Smiler's story was that the police raiding party on a launch sighted the camp just at daybreak and he and another boy crept

round to the rear of the six Aborigines with Nemarluk while Constable Don and others in the party completed the encircling movement.

Two days later, *The Canberra Times* noted that Nemarluk apparently was not badly injured by the fall, 'for he has completely eluded his pursuers.' The police, the report added, 'do not intend to continue the search unless further news of Nemarluk's whereabouts is revealed.'

The Melbourne *Herald* only got part of the story correct. What occurred was that Nemarluk was not at the Aboriginal camp but was found at a holiday camp run by Adams and Foster, two retired newsagents. Smile warily approached Nemarluk who jabbed at him with his spears. Smile then grappled with Nemarluk who, being the far more powerful man, broke away. Press reports claimed that Smile fired a number of shots from a revolver at the fleeing man and that he was hit in the back, but whatever the case, Nemarluk, 'half crawling, half limping,' disappeared into the mangroves.

His quarry gone, Constable Fred Don, or 'Fredon' as Pegasus dubbed him, returned to Darwin to face an outcry from residents critical at the ineptness of the police in trying to recapture Nemarluk. The *Northern Standard*, the only paper that used the word 'alleged' before 'murderer' in its reports, commented: 'If a sufficiently strong police force were not available why not call up a few specials? In the past the authorities have experienced no difficulty in securing 'specials' to oppose unemployed demonstrating in an endeavour to obtain better conditions, so a few of the 'specials' should have been 'roped in' to effect the arrest of an alleged desperate murderer.'

There is little doubt that Nemarluk was wounded in the fight with Smile. A report in *The Canberra Times* claimed Smile 'opened his head' with the butt of his revolver while another report stated that he had suffered a bullet wound in his left side 'which tore its way along a rib.' But 'torrential rains' heralding the onset of the wet season helped Nemarluk slip through a police cordon and head towards his tribal land at Port Keats. The special correspondent for the Melbourne *Herald* wrote:

> Police now admit that any further search in the jungle is hopeless and they do not intend to continue it until they receive word that Nemarluk has settled down. They consider that if Nemarluk was badly wounded by the last shot Smiler fired at him with his .45 police revolver, his only chance of life lies in the possibility that the Fitzmaurice River boys with whom he was camped will find him. If he was merely stunned by the fall, the masterly cunning which enabled him to elude the best bushmen in the police force for two-and-a-half years after the massacre of the three Japanese at Port Keats would make him a match against anything other than a surprise attack. He would be a grave menace to any policeman who came within range of his deadly spears, because he told the Fitzmaurice River boys that he would never be taken alive again, and would kill any policeman who tried to catch him. Constable Don is full of praise for Smiler's plucky attempt to hold his powerful and ferocious adversary. Such courage in tackling a man whose name is feared all along the north-west coast is almost unprecedented in an Aboriginal, he said.

An armed police party, headed by Constable McNab and comprising four native policemen, did set off in pursuit six days later, but was forced to return to Darwin due to heavy rain obliterating Nemarluk's tracks. Instructions were then sent to two policemen at Port Keats, Constables Tas Fitzer and Wally Langdon, who were investigating the deaths of two prospectors, Stephens and Kock, to 'keep a sharp lookout" for Nemarluk The two men, stated the *Canberra Times*, together with two other white fishermen, Fagan and Trayner, were 'believed to have met their deaths at the hands of the fierce Northern Territory natives.'

Meanwhile in Canberra, an agitated Minister for the Interior, Mr Perkins, telegrammed the Administrator in Darwin complaining that information was appearing in the press prior to receipt of his advice. 'Absence of official reports prior appearance information in the press most embarrassing,' the wire read.

The police, however, were not the only ones hunting Nemarluk. He was a notorious wife stealer who had made many enemies of men who were too afraid of his prowess as a warrior to challenge him openly. Some even enlisted the aid of tribal witch-doctors to destroy him by magic. They didn't succeed. But one morning he awoke to see five warriors, the scarlet sign of the pledged killers painted on their foreheads, creeping through the bush. Doubling behind them, Nemarluk hurled a spear that dropped the hindmost in his tracks. As the remaining four scattered, Nemarluk leapt at one, tumbled him into a gully and killed him. As the three remaining Aborigines hunted him, he lay hidden and killed them one by one as they came near.

Little was heard of Nemarluk for four months. One trick he learnt was to allow the police patrol to discover his tracks, then to hurry around in a circle behind them until he had cut the patrol's own tracks and sighted the police in front of him. This meant that when they stopped he could gain at least a little respite in sleep knowing that when the chase resumed the pursuers would start off in the opposite direction. Then, police received information that the 'Aboriginal murderer and jail breaker' was waiting near Legune Station with two stolen shotguns and a supply of cartridges the anticipated police pursuit party in the forthcoming dry season. Constable Langdon, who had been assigned to the case, was quoted as saying he was 'not disturbed by the news.' Nemarluk was much more to be feared if armed with spears.

A few weeks later, at 12.46 p.m. on March 8, 1934, an urgent telegram was sent by the Darwin Administration to the Minister for the Interior, Mr Perkins, in Canberra: 'Escapee Nemarluk arrested Leguna (sic) Station by trackers and now being escorted to Darwin.' Nemarluk had walked into a trap.

Legune Station is between the wide estuary of the Victoria and the border of Western Australia and it was here that one of the great police trackers, Bul Bul, a tribal enemy of Nemarluk who had constantly dogged his trail and two other Aborigines, Lippy Jack and Larry, from Auvergne Station, in those days owned by Connor, Docherty and Durack, a Perth pastoral firm, a hundred kilometres away, laid in wait. Bul Bul later told police what occurred. The three trackers had discarded their clothes and were in the native camp at Legune masquerading as bush natives when Nemarluk strode boldly into the camp seeking tobacco. Bul Bul immediately grabbed him and, helped by Lippy Jack, snapped on a pair of handcuffs. They then set off for Auvergne Station where they were to meet up with two policemen, Constables Tas Fitzer and Gordon Birt.

Fitzer and Birt had immediately set out on the seventy kilometre journey from Timber Creek, where the former was officer-in-charge, when news of Nemarluk's capture reached them. Birt, coincidently, had only arrived from Darwin the night before, replacing Langdon who had been transferred to another bush station. Fitzer and Birt were old friends and that night, together with Fitzer's wife, Jean, who before her marriage had played the piano for the Don Pictures in the days of silent movies, swapped news and shared a bottle of whisky that Birt had brought along to celebrate his thirtieth birthday.

Meanwhile, Nemarluk made a last desperate attempt to escape. It is probable that what happened was told by Nemarluk to Ion Idriess who said in his book that he knew the tribal leader personally, but in any event it was corroborated, in a briefer version, by Bul Bul. Just before dawn as they camped on the bank of the Bullo River Nemarluk, his hands manacled, began edging his way to the river's edge. As he rolled over the bank, Bul Bul awoke and leapt at him. Idriess describes the scene in his final chapter:

> As Nemarluk hit the water Bul Bul was on top of him, Nemarluk's manacled hands snatching for Bul Bul's throat. To the splash the sleepers awoke, sprang for the bank. Nemarluk was dragging Bul Bul under. Bul Bul's hand snatched for his belt and gripped a spare set of handcuffs. In the nick of time he swung the cuffs fair upon Nemarluk's head. They dragged Nemarluk back to the bank; the fight had gone out of him.

On arrival at Auvergne, the two policemen hurried to inspect the prisoner who was in a shed closely guarded by his captors. Secured by 'an ingenious arrangement of chains and handcuffs,' Birt remarked that even the great escapologist Houdini would have been baffled.

While camping near Victoria River Station on their three hundred and eighty odd kilometre trek from Auvergne to Willaroo Station where they were to hand Nemarluk over to Katherine police, Const Birt described an amusing incident. At the camp was an old friend and teamster, Burt Drew, with whom he was invited to have lunch and 'a few rums.'

> Some time during the afternoon Const Fitzer looked in and joined us in having a rum. Before leaving he

said to me, 'I will be at Victoria River Station tonight, Gordon, and the boys want to go to their camp. Will you stay and watch the prisoner,' Birt recalled. 'I replied in the affirmative and asked Tas whether he was having tea at the cattle station to which he replied, 'Yes.' After a few more rums Burt retired to sleep [and] I crawled underneath a wagon and in a moment was fast asleep. When I awoke it was dark and except for a shrill chorus of tropical frogs, almost complete silence reigned. I crawled out from underneath the wagon and saw a small fire burning at the police camp. My head ached and I was tortured with a thirst as I made my way towards the fire. I heard a mopoke call and the tinkle of a horse bell in the distance. Sitting by the fire was a figure whom I took to be one of the trackers. No doubt the others were visiting the local native camp. 'Where is the water bag?' I asked. 'Water over here,' replied the native indicating a waterbag hanging from a tree. I drank long and deeply and said, 'By Jove I was dry. Rum is no good.' 'Yes,' the Aborigine replied, 'grog is no good to anyone.' I could not figure who he was and said, 'Is that you, Bul Bul?' 'No I am not Bul Bul,' came the reply. 'Ah, then it must be Nugget.' 'No I am not Nugget.' 'Well, who are you then?' 'Me Nemarluk.' 'What, here all by yourself? Where are the others? 'They're all up at the camp' (meaning the big Aboriginal camp near Victoria River Downs). Next morning I said to Const Fitzer, 'I think Nemarluk is resigned to his fate and wouldn't run away if he could. 'Why?' Tas asked. 'When I got back here last night from Burt Drew's the prisoner was alone in the camp. And look at that sapling he is chained to. You can't tell me he couldn't have freed himself if he wanted to.

That afternoon, the two policemen and the trackers continued their journey, their prisoner, 'tall and agile, naked except for a loin cloth, striding alongside' and cheerfully helping to look out for goanna tracks for, having exhausted their meat supply, they sought the reptiles for food.

Waiting for Nemarluk when he finally arrived by train from Katherine at the two-and-a-half mile railway siding south of Darwin were three police constables, McNab, Heathcock and Langdon and about thirty curious onlookers. Manacled to Constable Heathcock, he is alleged to have said: 'Now, finish. No more fight. No more walk about, only jail.' On the drive to Fannie Bay Jail, he chattered with Constable Langdon, telling him how he narrowly escaped capture by Langdon three months previously when the policeman was returning from the Fitzmaurice River country after capturing his brother, Tiger, and seven of his fellow tribesmen wanted for the killing the prospectors Kock and Arinski. He managed to get away because he had left his tribe to go searching for wild bees' honey at the time Langdon raided his camp. Langdon later said he also told him that, after his escape from Fannie bay Jail he hid in the mangroves for several days until the search for him was abandoned and then made his way a hundred and fifty miles around the shores of the harbour to Delissavillle where waited several weeks for an opportunity to free his two lubras who were being held at the Darwin compound. After his fight with Smile and his fall over the cliff, he made his way back to his own country, resting a while at the Finness River.

Reporting Nemarluk's capture under the heading, 'Prison Bars for Nemarluk, the special correspondent for the Melbourne *Herald* wrote on March 22, 1934: 'When Nemarluk's trial is over next month, there will be a big exodus of Fitzmaurice River Aboriginal witnesses from Darwin where they have been held and supported for more than two years while police were chasing their elusive tribal overlord.'

The police lost no time in bringing Nemarluk before the Supreme Court on the charge of murdering Owashi and on April 10 – a little over two weeks after he was brought to Darwin – Judge Wells sentenced him to hang. During his trial the accused remained silent, steadfastly refusing to enter a plea. The only evidence against him was given by his two wives who had been kept in detention in Darwin for eighteen months.

Six days before Nemarluk was due to be executed, a successful appeal was made to the Secretary, Attorney-General's Department, Canberra, by the Chief Protector of Aborigines of the Territory, for the commutation of the sentence to life imprisonment, the commutation being approved at a meeting of the Federal Executive Council on May 2. The Chief Protector's grounds were that Nemarluk, 'an uncivilised Aborigine, had not been in contact with white civilisation and was wholly ignorant of the civilised British code' – sublime irony when one considers how the 'British code' treated the Aborigines in Tasmania. The Protector pointed out that there had been five lubras on board the lugger *Ouida* at the time of the killings, and that five other Aborigines found guilty of murder on the *Ouida* the previous year also had had their death sentences commuted to life.

The police practice of 'holding' lubras as principal, or even sole witnesses, already had come to the notice of the Australian Aborigines' Amelioration Association, an organization based in Perth, which, in a letter to the Prime Minister, said 'such women's evidence in many cases [is] obtained by intimidation or cruelty. Signed by the honorary secretary, Mr N Micklem Morley, the letter continued: 'Under British law a wife may refuse to give evidence against her husband; when dealing with natives this point is not only overlooked, but in certain cases lubras are 'held' by the police as decoys, it being known that a native's loyalty to his women will lead him to endeavour to secure their release. Will you please,' Mr Morley asked, 'inform me whether these practices have the sanction of your government and, if so, under what Act of Parliament, or Regulation, are they permitted. When witnesses are so 'held, are they chained together? If so, are they chained by ankles or neck? Under what Act of Parliament or regulation are the lubras Marpo (sic) and Nunnunnie being detained in Fannie Bay jail at the present time? Under what conditions are these particular lubras being confined?

A copy of Mr Morley's letter apparently was sent to the Department of the Interior and then forwarded to the Superintendent of Police, Mr A V Stretton. Mr Stretton's response was swift. No, he said in a report to the Administrator in Darwin, Lieut-Col R H Weddell, it was not the practice of police to hold lubras of accused Aborigines as decoys. There was no record of the police ever having resorted to this practice. His report continued: 'The question of the admissibility of the evidence of tribal wives against Aborigines has been repeatedly queried by learned Counsel representing accused Aboriginals. In every instance the objection has been overruled by the trial judge. All Aboriginals charged before the Supreme Court are represented by learned Counsel.'

Mr Stretton said there was no ground for Mr Morley's suggestion that evidence is obtained from lubras, in many cases by intimidation and cruelty. It was up to Mr Morley to substantiate his statement. It also was not the practice to chain witnesses. However, in certain circumstances it became necessary to prevent them absconding at night and in such cases special handcuffs permitting freedom of movement were used. Referring to Marpoo and Nunnunnie, Mr Stretton denied they had been detained in Fannie Bay Jail. 'These lubras are, with other witnesses, in residence at the Compound where they are living in contentment with other members of their tribe and are under no restraint whatsoever. The lubra Marpoo is the mother of a half-caste infant and would be required to remain at the Compound until the child were weaned, even though she were not a witness.'

Mr Stretton, however, did concede that on two occasions following the escape of their tribal husband, Nemarluk, Marpoo and Nunnunnie were locked in a dormitory with other lubras 'for one night on each occasion,' this precaution being taken 'in consequence of information being received that Nemarluk intended to raid the Compound and remove his lubras.' Mr Stretton said he had shown his report to the Chief Protector 'and he concurs with it.'

Even Administrator Weddell, on receiving a copy of Stretton's report, immediately wrote a letter to the Secretary of the Department of the Interior, saying that the report 'shows that Mr Morley has been in receipt of misleading or false information.'

However, Superintendent Stretton wasn't being entirely truthful. Marpoo and Nunnunnie had been kept in custody for an extraordinary lengthy period and in all probability yearned to return to their tribal lands. There is no evidence they were 'living in contentment' in the Compound. And it was hardly likely that police officers would publicly reveal they had used Aboriginal wives held in captivity as decoys. It was well known that no Aboriginal warrior worthy of his name would flee and leave his women, if he could possibly help it. In addition, even allowing for Press exaggeration, there must have been quite a number of Fitzmaurice River Aborigines who also had been kept in detention if there had been 'an exodus' after Nemarluk's trial.

As for accused Aborigines being represented by 'learned counsel,' this was not always the case. Quite often they were represented by non-qualified people. Mr Stretton was correct is stating that it was not the practice to chain witnesses. Nevertheless, chains were used on Aboriginal prisoners. A letter to Senior Constable Reid, who was stationed at Tenant Creek, signed by Sergeant J C Lovegrove, of The Northern Territory Administration, Alice Springs, states: 'I am forwarding, by the first available means, sixty feet of light chain for use on Aboriginal prisoners. The Minister directs that chains are only to be used on Aboriginal prisoners when they are being brought in from the bush to jail, or on such occasions as their use is considered absolutely essential for the safe custody of the prisoner until he is placed in jail. It is suggested that the portion of the chain around the neck of the prisoner should be padded with basil. Therefore, please place your requisition for basil at an early date. The sixty feet of chain is in three lengths of twenty feet each. If the occasion aris-es, one of these lengths may be cut in halves to make two ten feet lengths. Further cutting of the lengths is to be strictly avoided.'

The Rev John Sexton, honorary secretary of the Aborigines' Friends' Association in Adelaide also queried the detention of Marpoo and Nunnunnie. During the hunt for Nemarluk he asked the Minister for the Interior, Mr Perkins 'to give instructions for the return of the two women to their tribe.'

'According to reports,' he wrote, 'police hold out no hope of capturing Nemarluk, and this being so we should like to see the women returned by the police to their tribe and not simply released in Darwin where they might have considerable difficulty in reaching their own people in the Fitzmaurice River. Perkins replied that it was proposed to keep the women, for the present, in the Compound 'where they are contented in anticipation of re-arresting Nemarluk 'If Nemarluk is not re-arrested within a reasonable time, the women will be repatriated to their own country and will not be released in Darwin.' Nemarluk's two wives as well as 'other witnesses' were, of course, still in custody six months later.

There is also no evidence that N Micklem Morley 'concurred' with Superintendent Stretton's report. In a second letter to the Prime Minister a month later (November 14, 1933) he said that no attempt had been made to reply to 'the serious matters referred to.' He reminded the Prime Minister of his recent statement that 'the Commonwealth Government has accepted the guardianship of the Aborigines in the Northern Territory as a sacred trust and is doing everything in its power faithfully to carry out its obligations in that respect. It challenges any persons to produce evidence that the Aborigines of that territory are not properly cared for, or that when an irregularity has been brought to notice prompt and adequate action in the interests of the natives has not been taken.' Mr Morley continued: 'We have just been advised from England that Hon. S M Bruce had consented to receive a deputation in London, the object being to ask for an independent committee of inquiry into the condition of Aborigines in the Northern Territory. The opinion of my association is that this matter should be dealt with in Australia by Australians. If we fail to receive a satisfactory reply we regret that we can only assume that the practices referred to' (in his initial letter) 'are not sanctioned by Parliament and that the detention of the lubras Marpoo and Nunnunnie was illegal.'

Nemaluk's conviction was a foregone conclusion – he was deemed to be a killer long before he was brought to trial. Police had issued a warrant for his arrest without formal depositions being made. Throughout his trial he remained silent; nothing was put in his mitigation. The evidence of the two main witnesses – his wives – was not compellable. Not only that, but their identical statements, taken about eighteen months after the alleged murder, were never challenged. They had been kept in confinement in Darwin, under police surveillance, and not allowed to return to their tribal land. The bodies of the Japanese were never found. The statutory declaration of the *Ouida*'s agent saying the vessel had sunk and the Japanese drowned was never tendered. Nor, it appears, was the report of Sergeant Bridgland who had 'not the slightest doubt' that there were 'no suspicious circumstances.' Three Melville Islanders were on the vessel, but only one made a deposition. That, too, was taken long after the event and not challenged. There is also evidence that missionaries were concerned about Nemarluk's influence and fears were expressed publicly, particularly by a Brother Pye, that the tribal leader and his Red Band wanted to unite the tribes and drive them out of the Territory.

Nemarluk's one-day trial on April 10, 1934, was based on the evidence presented at the committal hearing, his two wives being the main Crown witnesses. 'A very large crowd assembled at the court,' wrote the correspondent for the *Canberra Times*. Heavy rain fell shortly after the trial began which 'compelled a pause in the proceedings as the noise and wind made the witnesses inaudible.' No submissions were made on Nemarluk's behalf, the jury quickly returned a verdict of guilty and Judge Wells promptly pronounced sentence of death.

Constable Birt always remembered Nemarluk, not as a grim and fearsome person as many believed, but as a happy smiling figure who marched for miles chained and shackled, through heat, bog and flooded rivers without complaint. Writing for *The Territorian* newspaper thirty-three years later, he recalled that six months after Nemarluk's incarceration, he had occasion to deliver three natives, sentenced for unlawful possession of beef, to Fannie Bay Jail. 'I stood inside the exercise yard waiting while the warrants were examined. The three prisoners sat together, self consciously, on a form, watching other native prisoners playing about. One tall Aborigine left a group and approached me, holding out his hand. I shook hands while he enquired after my health, and then rejoined his companions. 'Who is that?' I enquired from a passing guard. 'Don't you know him? That is the famous Nemarluk,' he replied. 'Fancy that, and I didn't know him. What a difference a haircut, shave and clean clothes makes.' Nemarluk died shortly before the Pacific War broke out. The other four convicted with Nemarluk for the murder of the Japanese were released in February, 1942, after Japanese aircraft attacked the jail during Darwin's first air raid. Paradoxically, the jail gates were thrown open by order of His Honour, Mr Justice Wells. Among other Aborigines released was Nemarluk's tribal brother, Tiger. He spent the war years as a houseboy in a Darwin residence but later returned to the Wild Lands, stole a lubra and was speared to death by the woman's husband. Aboriginal tracker Bul Bul served in the army and was killed in a motor accident in 1945. Tas Fitzer became a legend in the Territory. He led a varied life, having been a soldier in a small garrison on Thursday Island before he joined the Northern Territory police force. He eventually retired to Sydney where he died in 1966.

The last of the great Aboriginal warriors was buried in an unmarked grave, probably just outside the perimeter fence of Fannie Bay Jail. Nemarluk Drive, however, is named after him.

# Sources

Douglas Lockwood, *The Front Door*, Darwin 1869-1969

Ion Idriess, *Nemarluk*, First published in Australia by Angus and Robertson, 1941

Gordon Birt, 'Journey With Nemarluk', *The Territorian*, December, 1967

John Reed, *Peace of Mind*, Geneva Press, 1979

National Archives of Australia

Department of the Interior File of Papers

*The Territorian*

*Sydney Morning Herald*

*The Age*

*Canberra Times*

*Herald*, Melbourne

*Sun*, Sydney

*Northern Standard*

# JUDGE WELLS AND
# THE CALEDON BAY MURDER

It wasn't long after Nemarluk was sentenced that demands were made for the dismissal of Judge Wells. The event that sparked the outcry against His Honour was known as the Tuckiar case and involved the fatal spearing on August 1, 1933, of Constable Albert McColl, who, it was alleged, had raped Djaparri, one of Tuckiar's wives – an unlikely claim, although at the time Djaparri was in the policeman's custody. Constable McColl was a member of a police party sent to investigate the killings in September 1932 of five Japanese trepang fishermen by Yolngu Aborigines (sometimes, erroneously, referred to as Balamumu) at Caledon Bay in the newly created Arnhem Land Aboriginal Reserve when he was speared on Woodah Island.

Whether the killings were in revenge for the abuse of women, or the mistreatment of Yolngu workers, is unknown. But both Caledon Bay and Woodah Island to the south were recognised as two of the worst trouble spots in the Territory. Before the events of August 1, Yolngu tribesmen had killed two white trepangers named Traynor and Fagnan on board their boat after  Djaparri, Tuckiar's wife, had gone on board (either voluntarily or was abducted) and had intercourse with them. When news of Constable McColl's death reached Darwin, and with the Japanese Government demanding action be taken, the Government Resident, or Administrator, Lieutenant Colonel Weddell, who appears in the previous chapter, told the Minister for the Interior, Mr T Perkins, that a 'punitive' expedition was needed and, in a coded telegram to Canberra, called for a party of twenty-four men 'armed with 20 rifles, 2000 rounds of ammunition, 12 revolvers and 1000 rounds of ammunition and four shotguns and 300 cartridges.' The

Administrator's overreaction resulted in 'a strongly adverse public opinion', the word 'punitive' thought to have dire connotations, and the proposed expedition eventually was abandoned. Instead, a peace party comprising missionaries was sent to the tribal land of the Yolngu.

By adopting 'friendly and peaceful means,' as the *Age* newspaper put it, the party persuaded four men who confessed to killing the Japanese and a fifth, Dhakiyarr Wirrpanda, better known as Tuckiar, who allegedly confessed to spearing McColl, to return with them to Darwin where, despite protests by the Rev Alfred Dyer, second-in-charge of the Church Mission Society's expedition, they were immediately arrested.

The Melbourne *Herald*, on April 10, 1934, reported that there had been a sharp conflict of opinion between the missionaries and the police as to whether two of the Aborigines had intended to surrender to the police or to the mission expedition. There was also considerable doubt whether Tuckiar intended to surrender to police or to the mission. The next day, under the headlines, 'Pitiful Scenes in Darwin,' and 'Struggle in Terror When Handcuffed,' the *Herald* reported that the five accused men had been 'terrified by the procedure when they were arrested and locked up last night.' The report continued: 'Today, they were so terrified of the police that they had to be dragged forcibly from the lockup to the courtroom. When they saw some handcuffs they yelled piteously for the Rev Dyer who brought them to Darwin yesterday. Later when he appeared they clung to him. They struggled strenuously before they were torn apart.' The story concluded with the comment: 'When the natives offered to accompany the [mission] party to Darwin it was obvious that they had no suspicion that they might be called upon to answer for their actions in killing white men – in total ignorance of white man's law and in a country where the Aborigines recognised no law but that of their own tribe.'

*The Age* corroborated the *Herald's* story, its correspondent writing: 'Once in confinement all the arrested natives evidenced the utmost terror, exhibiting fear and shaking the bars of their cells like newly caged animals. They were almost utterly terrified by the proceedings in court.' The newspaper went so far as to write an editorial: 'When the missionaries established contact with groups of natives in Caledon Bay they met with men who volunteered confessions of complicity in the killings. This was distinctly embarrassing, as members of the [mission] party had been at pains to impress upon the tribesmen that their purpose was but to establish goodwill and unsuspecting contacts. Indeed, before setting out from Melbourne its leaders said they would neither do police work nor make their activities subserve police action in a preliminary way. The propensity of the Aborigines to make statements in assumed compliance with deference to the wishes of their interlocutors has been noted by many inquirers. Some explanation or assurance might be due to the Japanese Government, but the latter would realise the difficulties of dealing with a savage mentality to which the normal processes of a civilised criminal jurisprudence are utterly intelligible.'

None of this was given any weight by Judge Wells. Finally brought before His Honour, the four Aborigines were each sentenced to twenty years jail while Tuckiar was sentenced to death. No doubts had been raised about the judge's attitude towards Aborigines – and that perception of antipathy was inevitable. As in the case of Nemarluk, the evidence against Tuckiar was circumstantial and contradictory. However the judge took the view that the accused 'despite the fact that the evidence is very scanty, killed McColl in a deliberate and cunning way.' Ridiculing the claim that McColl had raped one of Tuckiar's wives, the judge continued: 'I am certainly of the opinion that it should not be allowed to go out amongst the Aboriginal population that an Aboriginal can murder a policeman and get away with a few years imprisonment. The white population seems to be impressed with that fact. I cannot find any reason at all for doing other than pronounce sentence of death.'

Again there was a public outcry and meetings were held condemning the sentence. The pressure built up to such an extent that the government, in October 1934, agreed to an appeal to the High Court that, after a ten-day hearing, unanimously quashed the conviction. Expressing its deep concern at the conduct of the trial, the court said comments by Wells were alone sufficient to render the conviction bad while his charge to the jury (he practically invited them to find a verdict of guilty) made a fair trial even less likely. As for Tuckiar's counsel, he failed to argue the case in favour of a complete acquittal or conviction for manslaughter. A new trial 'under fair conditions to the accused would be impossible.'

But some good did, after all, come as a result of the uncompromising and racist attitude of Judge Wells. Eminent academics in the south began to take notice. After the trials of Nemarluk and Tuckiar, Professor A.P. Elkin, who occupied the Chair of Anthropology at Sydney University, in an outspoken and enlightened article published in the Melbourne *Herald,* said the recent cases in Northern Australia, in which Aborigines were concerned, 'remind us that the relationship of the Aborigines to law is an important practical matter. But it is also an unsolved problem and it is such mainly because no sincere attempt has hitherto been made to frame and apply laws which have any real bearing on the special conditions of Aboriginal Australia.' He went on: ' Now, however, public opinion is very much interested in the question: resolutions are being passed with great frequency by social, scientific and humanitarian organizations urging the Government to make the processes of the law operate with a greater degree of common sense and justice than seems to be the case at present.' Professor Elkin said it was obvious that an Aborigine could not, from his point of view, have a just trial in a white man's court, unless he had attained such a degree of British civilization that he understood its view-point regarding various offences, as well as the language and methods of those courts. 'But,' he continued, 'there are hardly any full blood Aborigines in that position. The vast majority who are brought to trial discover, perhaps, not very clearly, that they are breakers of the laws of which they know nothing and which have no relation to their own laws and customs. They are tried in a language which is foreign to them while the judge, or magistrate, and barris-ters all talk in a foreign language, or an inadequate pidgin. What they do is to endeavour to sense what the judge and questioners would like them to say, and then they answer accordingly.' It was, said the professor, essential that the judicial officer conducting the trial must possess an ade-quate working knowledge of Aboriginal psychology, social organisation and law.

To ride roughshod over all this and merely to treat native offenders as offenders against white law is as unjust as it is ridiculous. And yet it happens. In one case an Aborigine was sentenced to ten years with hard labour for manslaughter, having killed a native one evening in a camp row during which missiles were thrown. Now his harsh sentence, which probably would not have been inflicted on a white man similarly accused, was justified by the pro-nouncement that Aborigines must be taught not to act in this way. Camp rows, especially at dusk such as the one referred to, are fairly common and there is always the risk of weapons being thrown.

In his book *This Whispering In Our Hearts*, historian Henry Reynolds summed it all up: 'The High Court's criticism [by Judge Wells] reached beyond the conduct of the trial to the attitudes and behaviour common in the Territory and in other frontier districts where the judicial system had never been able to deal fairly with the Aborigines. Individuals were always treated as representatives of their race. They were not so much people as examples. Political points were more important than impartial justice. The courts were places to affirm white dominance and settler solidarity. It was obvious that Justice Wells was determined to convict Tuckiar for murder. It was important that the blacks be given the lesson in court that interfering southerners had disallowed in the bush. Honour, respect and security were all at stake.'

On November 10, 1934, the day after he was released from Fannie Bay jail and taken to Kahlin Compound, Tuckiar disappeared. Rumour had it that he was shot by police and his body dumped in the harbour.

His face stares at you from an old photograph; he is a good looking man, with deep set eyes, wide mouth and curly hair. But he has a curious look, one, possibly, of deep sadness, or of bewilderment. Perhaps he has a premonition that he will never return to his tribal land. Tuckiar's case has been the subject of books and dramatisations and although his fate has remained a mystery there was a unique sequel.

On June 28, 2003, at a reconciliation ceremony in Darwin, Tuckiar's descendants publicly thanked Australia's Chief Justice, Justice Murray Gleeson, for the High Court's decision almost seventy years previously that his trial had been 'grossly unfair' and that it had been characterised by many procedural errors and many substantive injustices.' A ritual symbolising the cleansing tides of a huge tidal surge was followed by the installation of mortuary poles, painted by leading artists from Arnhem Land, in the Supreme Court, symbolising that Tuckiar's spirit was finally laid to rest.

# Sources

*The Age*, Melbourne

*The Herald*, Melbourne

*The Northern Territory News*

Henry Reynolds, *This Whispering In Our Hearts*, Allen and Unwin, 1998

Hugh V Clarke, *The Long Arm*, A Biography of a Northern Territory Policeman, Roebuck Society Publication No 12

# 'BRITISH JUSTICE' AND
# THE JAPANESE LUGGERS

Judge Wells took little notice of the criticisms from the south over the Tuckiar case and, ignoring demands that he resign, remained on the Bench. Then, in 1938, despite the fact that Japan had been on a semi-war footing since the previous year, he made another contentious ruling, this time involving Australia's national security and which was certainly not in the interests of the country.

In June the previous year and acting both under the Aboriginal Ordinance 1918-1937 and under instructions from the Administrator, Charles Abbott, Captain Charles Theodore Haultain, an experienced seaman and skipper of the Territory's (at that time) one and only patrol boat, *Larrakia*, made his first arrest of a Japanese lugger, the *Takachiho Maru No 1* that was allegedly within Territorial waters. At the time it was known that Japan was on a semi war footing. Haultain's job was threefold: to attempt to stop the lucrative lubra trade (the hiring by older Aboriginal men of their young and numerous wives to lugger crews had reached alarming proportions, much to the annoyance and frustration of the missions), to initiate an air sea rescue service from Darwin and to deal with trespassing by Japanese pearling luggers, some of which were suspected of spying, on Australia's north coast.

The crew of the *Takachiho* were taken off the boat and sent to the pearling grounds in another lugger before it was brought to Darwin. Within a month a second Japanese lugger, the *Dai Nippon*, was arrested and brought to Darwin and a few weeks later, a third, the *Tokio Maru*, was also arrested. Although the boats had become government property, and the period allowed to indicate intention to sue had long passed, the Japanese owners were granted special permission to take the matter to the

Supreme Court of the Northern Territory in an action for their recovery. As a result Charles Abbott and Captain Haultain found themselves as defendants.

Despite authoritative evidence by the prosecution that the Japanese were guilty (the Federal Government had passed an Act under which any vessel trespassing on the coast forming part of an Aboriginal reserve would be liable to arrest and escort to Darwin where it would be impounded), the judge found in favour of the Japanese, making it clear that not only did he accept the repeated explanations and denials of the plaintiffs, but that he was unimpressed with the demeanour of Captain Haultain who, he believed, had been impulsive and careless with his log book entries. Peter Elder, author of Judge Wells' potted biography, wrote that the lugger cases were a 'triumph' for the judge. 'He had embarrassed [Charles] Abbott [the Administrator with whom he had maintained a stormy relationship] and had ruled properly in law since the Commonwealth decided to take matters no further [in the light of] a submission to the Attorney-General [R G Menzies] that an appeal would probably fail on the point of law regarding the denial of innocent passage and the fact that the demeanour of the Japanese witnesses remained unshaken under cross examination. The self assurance of Captain Okishima was demonstrated when he was asked which European of the arresting party had brandished a revolver at him, he replied, 'every white man's face looks the same to me.' Significantly, Menzies subsequently wrote to Wells 'suggesting he should desist from further criticism of the Executive's discharge of its functions.'

The Japanese were awarded combined damages of two thousand, six hundred and seventy-two pounds and the Court ordered their vessels and pearl shell to be returned to them. Somewhat ironically a southern newspaper commented on the verdicts in an article headlined, 'Triumph of British Justice.'

The verdict obviously rankled in Captain Haultain's mind long after the case was over. Writing in his retirement thirty years later, he asked himself how the case could possibly have been lost. Those 'poor ignorant fishermen, as the judge had described them, had 'outdid anything contained in the memoirs of the late Baron Munchausen, a pretty gifted liar himself.'

> It was all very mysterious and the only conclusions one could draw... was that the government was more concerned with placating the Japanese than upholding its national rights. Several issues could well have influenced its course of action and opinions; the underlying threat of reprisal by an all-conquering (at that time) Japanese Empire and a possible economic repercussion to trade between the two countries. Whatever the causes may have been, the results produced a despicable surrender to a distant threat. So ended two years of toil and tribulation – tossed into the trash can of political expediency.

The Administrator, Charles Abbott, who had becomes friends with Captain Haultain, whom he described as an excellent leader and first class sailor and navigator, was also unhappy with the outcome. It was, he wrote somewhat diplomatically, 'a shock and a disappointment.'

When war broke out, Captain Haultain joined the RAAF but was transferred to the Navy in 1942 to command the corvette *HMAS Lithgow*. He later joined a special service a few months before the war's end. Demobbed in 1946 he joined Customs for a brief period and then joined the Australian Shipping Board (later to become the Australian National Line) as Chief Officer. He was promoted to Master in 1949 and remained with the company until his retirement twelve years later. He had spent forty-nine years at sea. Judge Wells, to give him his due, elected to stay behind to lend authority to the civilian administration during the Japanese bombing of Darwin. He may well have pondered his decision to release the Japanese luggers and to award damages against his own country. Retiring from the Bench in 1952 after suffering a stroke, he died in Darwin Hospital two years later.

# Sources

C T G Haultain, *Watch Off Arnhem Land*, Roebuck Society Publication No 4 1971

David Carment and Barbara James (Eds.), *Northern Territory Dictionary of Biography Vol 2*, Northern Territory University Press, 1992

# THE 'FARCE' OF WHITE MAN'S LAW

The issues concerning the compellability of Aborigines' wives to give evidence against their husbands and whether the ordinary criminal law applied to Aborigines were raised in the early days of the colony. They were researched in a paper titled 'The Application of the Criminal Law to the Aborigines of the Northern Territory', written by the late Mr Justice Martin Kriewaldt. Delivered to the fifteenth annual conference of the Australian Universities Law Schools Association held in Perth in 1960, it gives an insight into judicial attitudes in the first seventy years of white man's law. It also implies there were a number of disagreements between himself and Judge Wells over the treatment of Aborigines.

From 1951 until his death nine years later, Justice Kriewaldt was judge of the Supreme Court of the Northern Territory and, as he admitted, sat on numerous murder cases during that time. He took a particular interest in crimes involving Aborigines and considered that Aboriginal customs were relevant factors in determining the punishment to be awarded in the case of an Aboriginal offender, but were irrelevant to the substantive question as to whether or not a crime had been committed. He took the view that an Aboriginal should never receive a more severe sentence than would be imposed on a white person for the same crime. In an introduction to the judge's paper, a colleague, Professor Geoffrey Sawer, former Professor of Law, Australian National University, wrote that Judge Kriewaldt had developed from his experience a view that Aborigines as a whole, or at any rate a considerable number of pure-blooded Aborigines, had a slightly different mental make-up from the white man or the part Aboriginal and that this created inherent and inescapable difficulties in applying British legal concepts to their affairs, even after they had had considerable contacts with white society. Before his sudden death he wanted to investigate more closely what anthropologists and specialists in Aboriginal languages had to say concerning the possibility of explaining to tribal Aborigines the abstract concepts and procedural devices of a sophisticated legal system.

The judge wrote that as late in the colonial period as 1860 attempts were made in Victoria to induce the Supreme Court to hold that Aborigines were not bound by white man's law while in the Northern Territory there had always been a substantial body of opinion, particularly in Alice Springs, that whites should not concern themselves at all with crimes committed by one Aborigine against another, whether those crimes had any connection with tribal laws or customs or not. Nevertheless, the Australian courts had consistently held that the whole of the law at any given time applied to Aborigines and whites alike, except to the extent that the legislature had seen fit to make difference or to allow exceptions.

The argument to differentiate between Aborigines and whites was put as far back as 1836 by counsel in R v Jack Congo Murrell, an Aborigine who was charged with the murder of another Aborigine. His lawyer demurred to the indictment, arguing in support of the demurrer that

> ... this country was not originally desert, or peopled from the mother country, having had a population far more numerous than those that have since arrived from the mother country. Neither can it be called a conquered country, as Great Britain was never at war with the natives, nor a ceded country either; it, in fact, comes within neither of these, but was a country having a population which had manners and customs of their own and we have come to reside among them; therefore in point of

strictness and analogy to our law, we are bound to obey their laws not they to obey ours. The reason why subjects of Great Britain are bound by the laws of their own country is that they are protected by them; the natives are not protected by those laws, they are not admitted as witnesses in Courts of Justice, they cannot claim any civil rights, they cannot obtain recovery of, or compensation for, those lands which have been torn from them and which they have probably held for centuries. They are not therefore bound by laws which afford them no protection.

The Court quickly put paid to the demurrer:

> ... although it might be granted that on the first taking possession of the Colony, the Aborigines were entitled to be recognised as free and independent, yet they were not in such a position with regard to strength as to be considered free and independent tribes. They have no sovereignty... If the offence had been committed on a white, he would be answerable, was acknowledged on all hands, but the court could see no distinction between that case and where the offence had been committed upon one of his own tribe. Serious causes might arise if these people were allowed to murder one another with impunity, our laws would be no sanctuary to them. For these reasons the court had jurisdiction in the case.

In a similar submission reported in the Melbourne *Argus* in September, 1860, that a dependant race may retain their immunity from the jurisdiction of the courts of the dominant race also was promptly dismissed. 'The jurisdiction of the court is supreme, in fact, throughout the colony, and with regard to all persons in it. It is not intended to decide that in no case might there be a concession to a subject race of immunity from the laws of the conquerors living among them,' the Chief Justice ruled.

The Victorian Supreme Court also gave rulings as to the admissibility of evidence of female Aborigines married according to tribal customs. Judge Kriewaldt earmarks the trial in 1861 of Neddy Monkey who, with three other Aborigines were charged with the murder of another Aborigine. A female Aborigine, called as a witness for the prosecution, claimed to be the lubra of the accused Neddy Monkey, telling the court she had been married to him for more than a year. Had she been a white woman she could not have been compelled to give evidence against her husband. The trial judge reserved for the opinion of the Full Court the question 'whether Sally was not to be deemed the wife of the prisoner Neddy Monkey and whether her evidence was properly admissible against him.' Speaking for the Full Court, Sir Redmond Barry, who was guaranteed a place in Australian history for sentencing another Ned to death, said:

> The courts cannot take judicial notice of the religious ceremonies and rites of these people, and cannot, without evidence of their marriage ceremonies, assume the fact of marriage. The word 'lubra', also, is not to be understood by the court without explanation or evidence. To assume because this person described herself as a 'lubra', and as married, that she was the prisoner's wife within the meaning of the Act, is assuming too much, without evidence of the meaning of the word 'lubra', or of the facts constituting marriage according to the rites and ceremonies of these people. Every witness is presumed to be testable until the contrary is shown; and it is not by the use of unexplained terms, or the

assertion of vague rites and ceremonies, that the general rules of evidence are to be broken down.

In the 1920s, Justice Ross Ibbotson Mallam made similar decisions in the Supreme Court of the Northern Territory. However, as Judge Kriewaldt notes, following these decisions (and before the trials of Nemarluk and Tuckiar) a direction was given, probably at a ministerial level, that a woman married according to Aboriginal customs to an Aborigine accused of a crime should not be called as a witness. The direction, as we have seen, was ignored.

Judge Kriewaldt confessed that he was certain no Aborigine who had appeared before him had understood the respective functions of judge, jury or witnesses, or had appreciated that the proceedings were directed to ascertain whether the evidence sufficed to establish beyond reasonable doubt that he was guilty of the crime alleged against him.

> The plain fact is that in the Northern Territory the trial of an Aborigine in most cases proceeds, and so far as I could gather, has always proceeded, as if the accused were not present. If he were physically absent no one would notice this fact. The accused, so far as I could judge, in most cases takes no interest in the proceedings. He certainly does not understand that portion of the evidence which is of the greatest importance in most cases, namely, the account a police constable gives of the confession made by the accused. No attempt is made to translate any of the evidence to him. If the rule requiring substantial comprehension of the proceedings were applied in the Northern Territory, many Aborigines could simply not be tried.

Another difficulty was the impossibility, in most cases, to explain to the accused the exact nature of the charge. The judge could not conceive how, either in pidgin English or a native language the words 'did feloniously and of your malice aforethought slay' could be conveyed to the accused. Of course the judge's associate could say to the accused, or ask the interpreter to say to him, 'Now, which way you talk? You talk you bin proper finish killem that dead feller?' (usually Aborigines avoid mentioning the name of the deceased person) or 'you talk you no more bin killem that dead feller? You talk you bin killem, all right, no more corroboree, you go Fannie Bay long time. You talk you no more bin killem them other boys and that constable come here and tellem that feller judge all about that trouble. You savvy that? All right. Now you tellem me, you bin killem that dead feller, or you no more bin killem?' It was doubtful, the judge said, whether that would suffice to explain the effect of a plea.

It appears from Judge Kriewaldt's paper that he did not altogether agree with his controversial fellow judge, Justice Wells. In a significant comment he wrote:

> The percentage of verdicts of murder as between cases heard by Wells J. and cases heard by me remained constant, but after I assumed office the percentage of acquittals decreased while the percentage of verdicts of manslaughter increased. The change was due, I think, (a) to a difference in point of view between Wells J. and myself as to the extent to which the judge should indicate to the jury the view he holds as to the proper verdict; (b) the inclusion of civil servants amongst those qualified to serve as jurors, thus decreasing the percentage of old residents on juries; and (c) a fairly liberal view taken by me of the circumstances which entitle a jury to return a verdict of manslaughter on the ground of provocation.

Judge Kriewaldt wrote that he only tried one case where, in his opinion, the accused Aborigine was aware that his action was contrary to white law and would entail punishment. 'I can,' he said, 'call to mind no [other] case where the accused Aborigine was aware that he was doing wrong according to white man's law, but nevertheless acted as he did for fear of tribal punishment if he failed to act. In a substantial portion of the cases I have tried the accused acted in accordance with the customs of his tribe, but would have realised that his actions would lead to punishment if he had stopped to think about this aspect.'

Forty years before Judge Kriewaldt's appointment to the Northern Territory Bench, Professor Baldwin Spencer, leader of a 'scientific party', was given the task of deciding, among other things, the fate of the Territory's thousands of Aborigines and to report to the Federal Government. Included in the issues he was to tackle was crime and punishment. 'During the past year [1911],' he wrote in his final report, 'I have been present in court whilst natives have been tried for various offences and have been much impressed with the unfair position occupied by Aboriginal prisoners compared with white men.' Difficulties arose because of the enormous number of Aboriginal dialects of which ' … no ordinary person can attempt to learn more than one or two' resulting in pidgin English being used in court. 'It not infrequently happens,' he continued, 'that Aboriginals are convinced of their own admission which they make without in the least realising that such an admission which may or may not be the strict truth, will send them to jail. It is also nothing short of ludicrous to go into court the day before a trial and see the farce being solemnly enacted of a barrister and constable putting a witness through his facings in the box preparatory to his appearance before the judge next day.'

Foreshadowing Judge Kriewaldt, Spencer recommended that 'no Aboriginal be allowed to plead guilty except with the consent of an official protector and no native should be convicted on evidence other than such as would serve to convict a white man accused of the same offence.' He also acknowledged that Aborigines would only recognise punishment within their own tribal customs. 'There are many deeds committed by wild natives which are crimes and often most serious ones under our laws, but are in strict accord with their own customs and it is manifestly advisable not to interfere with their customs so long as they are dealing with fellow tribesmen.'

It wasn't about the middle of last century that Aboriginal customary law, finally, was given some recognition in Territory courts, but its application in an existing legal system was always a contentious matter. Instances of the involvement of tribal law were common. Trespasses into sacred areas, for example, were usually punished by death. Shortly after the Second World War, a Jaragba elder at Groote Eylandt 'spirited away' a number of young girls, taking them to a burial ground. For this reason, he was sentenced to death. (The girls later disappeared, never to be seen again). In another case, Durgaman, the Nangomiri (in the Daly River region) was the executioner when breaches of the secret cult of the bull-roarer occurred. Durgaman was credited with more than 30 ritual murders, but none of these were ever brought before the British court system. When customary law was taken into consideration, there were cases involving juveniles in which magistrates hesitated before releasing young offenders into tribal lands for punishment, particularly after an incident involving some youngsters from Wave Hill. Told by counsel that the offenders would be 'suitably chastised,' the court released them into the custody of some older tribal relations. Back at their settlement, they were shaved bald, bashed unconscious with stones and then 'bushed' for several weeks. In another early case, an Aborigine from Hooker Creek was charged with the murder of his brother. While under the influence of alcohol, the victim had poured boiling water on his brother's third and youngest wife, pushed her into a fire and then engaged in a prolonged fight with the accused who was sober. In fear of his life, the accused took up a heavy killing stick and with one blow dispatched his brother. He immediately took flight, well aware of the consequence – death. And so it proved. A meeting of elders decreed ritual death within minutes of the killing. Although the court acquitted the man when self-defence was raised, the death threat remained and he was unable to return to Hooker Creek. Four years later, the people of the settlement told the man's barrister they still planned to kill him. The case gave rise to considerable discussion and the question was raised as to whether white man's law should have been involved at all.

It is interesting to note here that some Aborigines became gainfully employed after being convicted of murder in the white man's court. For example, Sugarbag, who had a habit of clubbing unsuspecting miners on the head as they emerged from their mineshafts, and then stealing their food, was sentenced to death. The sentence was commuted, but after a relatively short period in jail he was released and got the job of washerman at the police barracks in Darwin, an appointment that must have occasioned a few sceptical glances. But Sugarbag carried out his duties diligently, despite the fact that he was suspected of sipping methylated spirits that was put in the iron he used on the police uniforms. Another case involved an Arnhem Land Aborigine named Coorapinni, alias Murdering Dick, who, after being convicted of killing a white man near the Winton River, escaped from Fannie Bay jail. Tracked by Constable Jack Stokes, the officer-in-charge at Maranboy at the time, he was found sleeping in a shed at a Chinese market garden on the King River and was escorted back to Darwin. When he was eventually released, Constable Stokes employed his as his tracker, an occupation in which he became renowned. Another Aborigine, Stumpy, convicted of fatally spearing his thirteen-year-old stepdaughter with a shovel spear, also became a well-known police tracker after his release.

# Sources

Justice Martin Chemnitz Kriewaldt, 'The Application of the Criminal Law to the Aborigines of the Northern Territory', *Western Australian Law Review*, Vol. 5, 1960

Tom Pauling, *Seminar on Aboriginal Customary Law*, 1976

Barbara James, *The Darwin Star*, Vol 4 No 48, 1979

Hugh V Clarke, *The Long Arm, A Biography of a Northern Territory Policeman*, Roebuck Society Publication No 12

# FORBIDDEN LOVE ON
# GROOTE EYLANDT

The Aboriginal clans of Groote Eylandt had the reputation of being the most aggressive and warlike in the Northern Territory. They had strict tribal law and payback was often resorted to. Payback was a word which confronted – and worried – judges in many a homicide. Should an Aborigine, after suffering payback at the hands of his tribe, again be punished in a white man's court? Alternatively, if punished in a white man's court, should he be subjected to payback on return to his settlement? And should those who carried out payback be brought to justice?

One of the more unusual cases came before Mr Justice Muirhead in the Darwin Supreme Court in 1982. The judge evidently had decided opinions on the question.

In the late afternoon of July 14 the previous year, two Aborigines armed with shovel-nosed fighting spears set out to kill a young member of their clan who had broken ancient and rigid tribal traditions. Calling on him to step out of his home where he lived with his mother, they launched their spears, but their intended victim dodged and they missed their mark. In retaliation he threw his own spears at his would-be killers, but they, too, missed.

The confrontation, on a road near the remote Angurugu Mission on Groote Eylandt in the Gulf of Carpentaria, climaxed a story of forbidden love that the tribe was determined at all costs to stop. It ended in death and the subsequent acquittal of a young man on a charge of manslaughter.

When the traditional spearing failed to achieve its purpose, the head of the clan, Mr Bob Bara, decided he himself would kill the man, even though he was his tribal son. Seizing a spear from a bystander, he loaded it into a woomera and hurled it at short range. But the young man again violently threw himself sideways and the two and a half metre weapon flew harmlessly past his stomach.

In the ensuing fight between the two men, Mr Bara received a spear stab in the back of the shoulder. Bleeding profusely he was eventually evacuated to Darwin Hospital where he died sixteen days later.

As a result, John Wurrabadalumba, twenty-one, a carpenter employed at the mission, was charged with his murder. At the outset of his trial, the Crown withdrew the charge and substituted manslaughter and Wurrabadalumba, also known as John Bara, pleaded not guilty.

The jury of nine men and three women listened intently as the Crown Prosecutor, Mr Tony Cavit, unravelled the tangled events that led to the confrontation.

John Bara, he said, had formed a relationship with a young woman by the name of Helen Warramabra. In fact, they had been in love since their schooldays.

But their relationship was frowned upon by the community for two reasons. The first was that they were cousins and too close in blood to be accepted. The second was that Helen's elderly husband had died shortly before the spearing incident.

Custom, Mr Cavit said, required that Helen remain celibate for a year after her husband's death. It also required the performance of certain ceremonies that would release her and allow her to go to another man – but not to her cousin.

Nevertheless, the two young lovers decided to spend a week in the bush together, which led the community elders to believe they had an intimate relationship.

On her return Helen, as part of her punishment, was speared through the hand and beaten with a heavy stick by her two sisters. She was seriously hurt and when police saw her she was semi-conscious, unable to speak or walk, and in great pain.

After Helen was assaulted the word got around to some of the men of the community and they decided that the friction was produced by her continued relationship with John Bara and that this should end, Mr Cavit said.

In records of interview with police that were read to the jury, John Bara recalled the spear fight. He said the two men told him to stand on the road and they would throw spears at him and then it would be his turn.

His testimony continued:

> They said, 'We are going to kill you.'
>
> They spread out and I stood in the middle. I asked if I could take them on one by one, but they started throwing their spears together. A lot of spears came at me. When they finished, I threw mine. Then Uncle Bob [his tribal father and clan leader] ran up with a spear. I jumped out of the way and it just missed my stomach. He ran past me, picked up the spear and tried to stab me. I jumped away again.
>
> He went past me again and as he did I pushed my spear in the back of his shoulder. He was going too far for me. He was out to kill me.

John Bara said as he walked up to his tribal father and pulled the spear out, a group of men armed with spears and sticks approached him. One swung a nulla nulla, hitting his hand and breaking his fingers. However, he managed to flag down a car driven by a mission employee and was taken into protective custody by the police.

When the Crown concluded its case, Mr Justice Muirhead directed the jury to acquit the accused.

'When the accused stabbed Bob Bara with his spear, it was in self-defence, as he was in peril of his life,' he said. 'At short range he [Bob Bara] made what can only be described as a sustained and dangerous attack on this young man. His actions in stabbing the man in the shoulder could not be classified other than being in reasonable self-defence.'

'It had been,' the judge added, 'a rather unusual trial.'

John Bara apparently didn't suffer any further payback when he returned to his clan. If he did, it was kept very quiet.

Stories of payback are legion, but perhaps one of the most tragic was related by patrol officer and protector of Aborigines, Syd Kylie-Little in his book *Whispering Wind*. It also involved forbidden love and happened in the late 1940s when Kylie-Little was on patrol in Arnhem Land. One evening a young man and a girl ran into his camp, obviously exhausted. It happened that the man was the girl's half brother and they had broken the laws of their tribe by making love and marrying at a mission station before returning to their tribal territory – a fatal mistake as the penalty for incest was death. Pursued by heavily armed members of their tribe who also arrived at the camp, the young couple took off again, Kylie-Little unable to stop them, or their pursuers from following, despite threatening them with his rifle. The following day the patrol officer and his assistants came across the young man's body, spears sticking out of it like porcupine quills. Nearby they found the girl's tracks leading into a river. Oondabund, Kylie-Little's assistant explained, 'They bin walkem longa river. Lookabout findem crocodile. Allabout bin makem lubra swim now. Finish.' They were probably the saddest words Kylie-Little heard during his career in the Territory. Nevertheless, he came to the same conclusion as Judge Muirhead – that there should be no interference with tribal law.

# Source

Syd Kylie-Little, *Whispering Wind, Adventures in Arnhem Land*, Hutchinson, London, 1957.

# GONE WITH THE WIND

They were good mates, Murray (Mo) McNaught and Lionel Curtis. They toiled together as construction workers in the blistering heat of the Northern Territory, swapped yarns and, at the end of the day, adjourned to that oasis of bonhomie, the Bushranger Inn at Adelaide River. But their friendship, as some friendships do over a period of time, started to sour and Mo began to throw his not inconsiderable weight around.

The catalyst was an argument over the value of a D-9 Caterpillar dozer owned by the Dussan Construction Company for which they worked. Mo said a hundred and fifty thousand dollars was the top price, but Lionel stoutly maintained that fifty-four thousand was nearer the mark. The atmosphere between the two men simmered all day but, as usual that evening, after receiving their pay, they stopped off at the Bushranger for their regular tinnies, albeit at different tables. Lionel was just about to take a sip of his beer when Mo approached him, dropped his trousers, turned, raised his leg and with the words, 'Cop this you bastard,' farted in his face. For a nanosecond, Lionel was stunned. He then threw his beer can onto the table, jumped to his feet and said, `You'll pay for that.'

Others in Lionel's group thought it was all a bit of a joke and gave an embarrassed laugh. Lionel, however, was certainly not amused. He ran out of the hotel, but returned a while later with a high powered rifle that he had borrowed from a mate of Mo's, one Reg Hackitt. Cradling the firearm in his arms, he approached Mo who had rejoined a group of men seated by the juke box. Then, as he neared his erstwhile friend, and 'looking angry and determined,' he raised the rifle and was heard to say, 'Now fart you bastard,' and pulled the trigger. Mo was hit in the left side of his chest, and, with blood spurting from the wound, he tried to rise from the table before collapsing onto the floor. He died shortly afterwards.

Later that night, thirty-five-year-old Lionel was found in an old house near the disused Adelaide River Railway Station and charged with murder. Initially the Crown had difficulty producing witnesses, nothing unusual in the Territory. One, so Lionel's committal hearing was informed, had gone fishing, another was in hospital and a third was a truck driver 'somewhere between Darwin and Alice Springs.' But eventually Magistrate Alisdair McGregor heard all the evidence, found a prima facie case and committed Lionel for trial before Mr Justice John Gallop. Lionel reserved his defence.

The relevant facts were repeated before His Honour. Reginald Andrew Hackitt said that on the night of October 12, 1979, he remembered Lionel saying to him: 'I'll fix Mo. I'll give him a fart in his face. And Senior Constable Harry Cox, of Adelaide River, said when he approached the accused, Lionel said: 'Yes, I shot the bastard. Is he dead? I'm sorry he's dead, but I'm not sorry I shot him.' 'I said: "Has be been giving you a hard time?" and he replied, "Yes, he thumped me twice in the last eleven days. I know I can't beat him. Then, last night he walked up to me and farted in my face. What would you do if a bloke farted in your face?"

'Well,' Constable Cox replied, 'I'd be upset.'

The jury took three-and-a-half hours to reach its verdict – not guilty of murder but guilty of manslaughter. But His Honour wasn't completely satisfied and took the unusual step of recalling them and asking the reason for their decision, despite an objection from Defence counsel, Geoff Eames. Even the Crown Prosecutor, Peter Tiffin, joined in, saying he had not considered that procedure and he was not aware of it having been done before in similar circumstances. The judge proceeded:

His Honour: Madam Foreman... are you able to tell me the basis upon which you found manslaughter instead of murder. There was an assumption on both sides, I think, that you would be satisfied beyond reasonable doubt of one or the other and you obviously have been. Now, can you tell me the basis upon which you found manslaughter"

The Foreman, 'The main basis was that we considered that Mr Curtis had not gone to the Adelaide River Inn with the intention of killing anyone. He was – he was obviously influenced by the amount of alcohol that he had consumed; he was also influenced by the provocation, between his relationship with McNaught.'

His Honour: 'I see.'

The Foreman: 'I think that would be the...'

His Honour, 'So it was based upon just, do I have it correct, Madam Foreman, that it was based upon a number of alternatives, namely absence of intent to kill or inflict grievous bodily harm, and you found that provocation existed as a matter of law, and therefore you were justified in reducing the crime from murder to manslaughter. There were really two bases – is that correct? You are nodding your head, would you mind saying yes or no.'

The Foreman: 'Oh yes, yes.'

His Honour: 'So there is no real consensus as to one or the other?'

The Foreman: 'No.'

His Honour: 'But by joint decision you decided upon manslaughter rather than murder?'

The Foreman: 'Yes.'

His Honour: 'Well, thank you Madam Foreman, ladies and gentlemen. I am sorry to have detained you; you are now free to go'

And Lionel? When, in due course, he came up before His Honour for sentence, he received three years imprisonment. And nothing was ever heard of him again.

# ALF'S OBSESSION AND
# FEARS OF LYNCHINGS

An intriguing sidelight of life in the Top End with its small population, was the number of people in prominent positions who, over the years, got themselves into trouble with the law. Most of the offences involved assault or occasionally, theft, although there was one stipendiary magistrate who was convicted of indecent exposure.

Now, one would expect a senior lecturer in law would not be other than law-abiding, but in 1978, things went awry for Alfred Horace Clothier. Not only was he found guilty of assault and malicious damage, but he also received a thorough dressing-down from the magistrate.

Alf, senior lecturer in law at Darwin's Community College, had pleaded not guilty to assaulting one Ted Baczkowski and wilfully and maliciously damaging property valued at thirty dollars. It was a two-day hearing during which evidence was given that Baczkowski and Lindy, his wife, and two young children took over Alf's flat in Smith Street, Darwin, while he was overseas. The arrangement had been made with Peter Anderson, a fellow lecturer of Alf's who was renting the flat but who, earlier in the year, had moved to other premises. The thrust of the prosecution case was that Alf allegedly had assaulted Mr Baczkowski with a champagne bottle and that he had threatened to 'permanently incapacitate' Anderson if he gave evidence against him, both allegations being vigorously denied by Alf.

During three hours in the witness box, Alf gave his version of the events. He said he believed Anderson to be a 'kind, courteous little fellow,' but he was unaware that he had a split personality. While Anderson had been 'toadying' to him and trying to 'win his friendship,' he had also been carrying tales to the principal of the college in an effort to get him dismissed. As for Mr Baczkowski, Alf described him as an emotional Slav, a remark that prompted the magistrate, Alisdair McGregor, to observe that he wasn't particularly keen on Anglo-Saxons. And when Alf remarked that he would not have objected if Mrs B Baczkowski had remained in his flat after her husband had left, refuting a claim that he had used objectionable language to her, Magistrate McGregor expostulated that it was a 'scandalous' thing to say. 'She is,' said Alf, 'a gracious lady, so I was courteous to her. I like to think I am a quiet and dignified man.'

Alf said he had gone to his flat to 'recapture his chattels' after arriving back from overseas. 'I must admit I was very agitated,' he said. 'My chattels were scattered. Anderson had also scattered my law books in a tool shed and cockroaches had eaten them. I had no clothes, my wife was coming up [from Adelaide]. My prime motive was to re-capture my chattels. I was in dire fear they [the Baczkowskis] would steal all my chattels. I noticed a lounge suite and three chairs had been removed. Baczkowski was there and his wife. I said: 'I'm not leaving the premises. I don't know you people, you are trespassers and potential thieves.'

Alf said Mr Baczkowski grabbed him by the arm and tried to drag him out of the flat. 'I am in very poor heath. I made seventy-four trips in the rear turrets of Lancaster bombers over Germany during the war and am on a fifty per cent disability pension. The dog was with Baczkowski and it joined in the fray. It was a complete mêlée. I rushed to the back of the room. Baczkowski hit me twice. He pushed me from side to side. I pushed him from side to side. The dog joined in as if he was enjoying it. The woman went running off to the police. I immediately got in my car and went to the police station.'

Cross-examined by the prosecutor, Ashley Macnay, Alf said Mrs Baczkowski had treated him very patronisingly, like a servant. 'The husband was very abrasive and regarded me as an interloper.' Asked if he had noticed glass fragments on top of the 'fridge – the remains of the broken champagne bottle – Alf replied: 'You don't look at things when you're being chased by an enraged Pole and a dog.' Later in cross-examination Alf admitted writing letters to the police commissioner Mr McAulay, Mr Pat Loftus, a Crown prosecutor and Sergeant Jack Nicol, a police prosecutor, as he was 'very unhappy' after being charged by summons.

Fining the learned lecturer a total of two hundred and forty dollars with five hundred and thirty-seven dollars costs, the magistrate said Alf's behaviour had been 'totally shabby and quite abhorrent to ordinary standards of society.' He had no doubt whatever that the evidence of the prosecution and not Alf's was to be believed.

'Some of the things I heard from you in the witness box have left me singularly unimpressed,' he told the chastened lecturer. 'I am not able to give any weight to the evidence of the defendant save that I do accept that he is a man concerned with his goods. It would be fair to say he is obsessed.'

About the time Alf was performing his antics, there was a case in which the Chief Judge, Mr Justice Forster, commented that the behaviour, 'if allowed to go unchecked,' of two well-known Darwin businessmen and stalwarts of the Lions Club, 'could lead to lynchings and all sorts of other things.' The two men, he said, had behaved like louts. The judge was hearing an appeal by the pair against their sentences of six months' hard labour for assault on the grounds that they were manifestly excessive.

Earlier, when sentencing the two men in the lower court, Magistrate McGregor said their actions 'were not that of the good Samaritan, the priest, or the Levite,' descriptions used by their solicitor in their defence. He said the circumstances of the assault were that the defendants, Desmond Judge and John Henley-Smith, both of Darwin, laid in wait for one, Clive Lane, at a demountable occupied by Lane's de facto wife, May who, her husband alleged, had been found in bed with Desmond Judge.

When Lane arrived, he was confined in a house and then taken by them to the Lions Park 'which I suppose,' said the SM, 'is, in a way, symbolic of you both being Lions at the time, though I say it does no credit to the organization.'

The magistrate went on: 'You then took him to the beach, forced him to strip off, made him go into the sea, brought him back from the sea, forced him to have a cold shower and took him to the home of a chap to whom he owed money. This man recommended that you return his clothes to him and you, Henley-Smith, gave him back the lead for his car.'

Mr McGregor said that Lane, on his oath, claimed he was kicked and that a wound on the back of his leg was opened. 'He has said on oath that he was threatened about his private parts by Mr Judge with a piece of cable – a thing which has been variously described, [but] it sounds to be quite a fearsome implement.' Addressing the defendants, the magistrate said, 'You also had the effrontery to tell me that you only made him take his clothes off because he did not smell nice. But you had the decency to admit that he might just have urinated in fear. I think that is extremely likely.'

Despite his forebodings of lynchings, Judge Forster allowed the appeals and reduced the terms of imprisonment from six to three months. 'The feelings I have,' he said, 'is that Mr McGregor became hostile to these yahoos taking the law into their own hands. It unbalanced his judgement somewhat.'

Lane was later convicted and sentenced in the Supreme Court to eight years' jail for attempting to murder May.

# THE IRREPRESSIBLE MISS PINK

Few things seemed more bizarre to the Territory's resident engineer, David (D D) Smith when he spotted a lone figure trudging across the middle of the harsh Tanami Desert with, as it turned out, a bag containing watermelon slung over the shoulder. At a distance he thought it was a mirage, but as he drew closer the apparition took the unmistakable form of a middle-aged woman wearing a long dress.

This is one of many anecdotes told about Olive Muriel Pink, one of the most extraordinary characters in a cavalcade of quirky individuals who have left their mark, indelible or otherwise, on the Northern Territory. In some ways, she was like a Bea Miles of the Centre, exhibiting many of the eccentric traits of that singularly odd but highly intelligent Sydney character that was the scourge of officialdom and police, not to mention taxi drivers, in the 1940s and 50s.

Espousing the cause of Aborigines long before it became fashionable, Miss Pink bombarded officialdom, from the Governor-General down, with a mountain of letters, often penned in ink of three colours with frequent arrows and sentences underlined for emphasis. Administrators, the judiciary, police, anthropologists, and a legion of public servants incurred her wrath, with one former Administrator sighing that she was capable of causing more trouble than a battalion of soldiers. Jock Nelson, another Administrator, told colleagues that when he was the Member for the Territory in the House of Representatives he built up a 'Miss Pink file' about a foot thick consisting of letters on a wide range of subjects.

Born in Tasmania in 1884, Olive Pink is believed to have attended a school run by Quakers. Later, she was employed as a commercial artist with the Public Works

Department and the then Railways Commission of NSW, but was retrenched during the Great Depression About this time she became interested in anthropology and studied anthropology part time at Sydney University and there is some evidence she had some dealings with the famous Daisy Bates. In her book *Daisy Bates* by Elizabeth Salter, the author mentions a 'jolly little artist called Miss Pink.'

During the 1930s Miss Pink, despite warnings that the Aborigines in the region were 'militant' and a European had been speared to death, roamed the Tanami Desert, on her own, carrying out anthropological studies, mainly among the Arrernte and Warlpiri people. For a time, she lived among the Warlpiri at Thomspon's Rockhole, and later at Yuendumu before moving to Alice Springs in the late 1940s. Her studies gave rise to an 'impossible dream' – she wanted Aborigines to be left alone without any change to their life style.

The anecdotes about her are legion. On one occasion she was travelling in the desert with a companion, Sam Irving. When they came to bed down for the night, Miss Pink pointed out to Sam that she carried a pistol for her protection. Sam replied, 'Miss Pink, your face is your protection.' She kept the pistol right up to her death. There were also confrontations with the law. A heavily built Alice Springs policeman often fell into her bad books. He was strolling along with another policeman who was somewhat lighter when Miss Pink spotted them and loudly announced to all and sundry as they walked by, 'Look at these two – they'd make a good advertisement for Ford Pills-before and after.' Alice Springs public servant Glen Thomas, hearing that Miss Pink was about to be switched through to his telephone, greeted her with a few lines from the song about Lily the Pink, who made medicinal potions during the Prohibition period. 'Don't be rude,' snapped Olive. 'I'll report you to Shylock' which was her name for his boss, Frank Dwyer, former Deputy Secretary of the

Department of the Northern Territory. She followed up the threat by asking who was this woman, Lily the Pink. When told that the Pink in question had made herself very popular by mixing alcoholic potions for boozers, Miss Pink remarked how clever she must have been, adding, 'I wish I could do something useful like that.'

The Territory's resident engineer at the time, the popular David Smith, recalled that he was travelling by utility across the desert to Tanami when he spotted a moving object on the horizon. As he approached, he was surprised to find the object developed a human form. It turned out to be Miss Pink. She was trudging across the desert in a full-length dress with a sugar bag over her shoulder and, on enquiry, said she was heading for Tanami, roughly a hundred and twenty kilometres away. As he was making for the same place, Smith invited her to join him but, despite the fact that she had known him personally for some years and also had many official dealings with him, she flatly refused. She said the bag she was carrying contained her only food and, on his asking what she was eating, she replied it was watermelon. Realising the seriousness of her situation he tried to escort her to his vehicle but 'she exploded like a tigress defending her young, scratching him on the face and hitting him over the head with the bag of watermelon.'

On another occasion she had no option but to accept assistance. Word was received that Miss Pink was ill at her camp in the Tanami and a rescue party was sent out from the Alice. On arrival they found her so ill she couldn't walk. A litter was made from saplings and flour bags and she was carried fifty kilometres over boggy ground to an 'old jalopy' for the four hundred odd kilometres trip along a rough track back to Alice Springs.

Miss Pink frequented the Alice Springs courthouse especially when cases against Aborigines were to be heard, and sometimes commented loudly when she disagreed with the Court's decision. She was highly indignant when convictions were recorded against two Aborigines in a tribal murder case that involved an appointed execution squad who donned special shoes made from feathers, blood and gum to hide their tracks. Jumping to her feet she made loud derogatory comments about 'so-called British justice' and continued on in a similar vein until the exasperated judge ordered her arrest. She was freed when, most reluctantly, she apologised. On another occasion she was convinced that the local lock-up was unsatisfactory and asked to carry out an inspection of the premises. Told this was not possible she committed a minor offence, refused to pay the fine and demanded to go to the lock-up instead. However, she was thwarted at the last minute when the officer in charge of the prison paid the fine himself.

Often wilful, even pig-headed, she was given an air conditioning unit for her hut in Alice Springs by local businessman, Reg Harris. At the time an Aborigine she had befriended had died and she wanted him buried as a 'heathen' without church rites. The Aborigine ended up being buried by the Catholic Church, much to Miss Pink's chagrin, for one of her pet hates was the Catholic Church. She blamed the unfortunate Reg Harris, sent back the air conditioning unit and bought another to replace it.

Her mercurial likes and dislikes were reflected in the trees she planted and tended with the aid of Aboriginal helpers in her arid zone flora research reserve. Every tree bore the name of some prominent citizen and if that person fell out of favour with her she stopped watering it. It was remarked that 'if the leaves of Mr Archer were drooping and the leaves of Mr Marsh were bright and green or Mr Barclay was growing vigorously, one knew at once what had occurred in the handling of her latest request or with whom she had had a row.'

Miss Pink often spoke of a 'special friend' who was killed at Gallipoli in 1915 and the portrait of a soldier in uniform hung above her bed for many years. She once con-fided she would like the portrait to be buried with her. The year before she died at the age of ninety-one, she said her reason for living had died at Gallipoli. The portrait was that of Captain Harold Southern, her intended fiancé who was killed at Gallipoli.

## Source

Northern Territory Newsletter, *Department of Northern Australia*, July and September, 1975

# THE CIB CHIEF AND
# THE MEAT CLEAVER

'It could only happen in the Territory' was an oft repeated comment. Certainly the case of the head of the Alice Springs CIB attacking a solicitor with a meat cleaver was rather bizarre, to say the least. Whether it was a practical joke or a 'frightening assault with malicious intent' was something the magistrate had to determine.

Gordon Pelletier was a tall, well-built, bombastic man with a wide smile who practised as a solicitor, mainly in the court of summary jurisdiction in Darwin. But one evening in 1979, much to everyone's amazement, while dining with some friends in an Alice Springs restaurant, he was attacked with a meat cleaver by, of all people, the chief of the Alice Springs CIB, Detective Sergeant Denver Marchant.

It was his intent, the detective later told the Alice Springs Magistrate's Court, to play a practical joke. But Crown solicitor, Andrew Kirkham, claimed that Detective Marchant had acted with malice and had felt 'antagonism and resentment' towards Mr Pelletier.

In evidence, the aggrieved solicitor said Detective Marchant had come to his table at the Chopsticks Restaurant seeking advice on a legal matter. When Marchant had used foul language he had told him to stop because there were ladies present, but the detective continued in the same course vein. When he suggested it was neither the time nor the place to discuss such matters, Detective Marchant replied, 'I thought you were my fucking friend.'

Mr Pelletier said he had taken the detective under the shoulder and escorted him to another table with the restaurant's manager, Eddie Wong. Later, while he was paying the bill for his party he remarked to Mr Wong that Denver was a nice guy when sober, but could become violent when drunk. Almost immediately he heard a door smash open and he saw Detective Marchant standing and clutching a meat cleaver.

Said Mr Pelletier: 'I believed he was about to kill me. I tried to scream, but my throat was paralysed. I guess I made a sort of croaking sound.' He tried to run away, but tripped and fell. As he did so, he saw the 'chopper' coming towards him. 'I became hysterical,' he had later told police.

But Detective Marchant had a different story to tell. He had not been upset with Gordon in any way on the night of the 'incident.' He had been coming back from the toilet when he saw Gordon paying the bill, noticed a dozen or so cleavers on a kitchen table and decided to play a joke on the unsuspecting solicitor. He had walked up behind him as he was leaving and said in a soft, slow voice, 'Hey, Gordon.'

'Gordon spun around and then started to run. He ran four or five steps before falling over. I stopped and said, 'It's only a joke' and he stood up and looked at me. Then Eddie Wong came out and asked me to give him the chopper. I heard someone mention the police and I thought, 'Jeez, I've blown it.' The detective said he then phoned the police station to tell them some people might be making a complaint about a practical joke he had played that had backfired. Later that night he had seen Gordon sitting in a car at the police station. He started to talk to him, but Gordon jumped out of the vehicle, kicked him in the stomach and ran into the police station.

Crown solicitor Kirkman said the detective's resentment had smouldered, fuelled by an increasing intake of liquor, and exploded into violence when he heard himself described as a person who was violent when drunk.

But solicitor, Mr Ted Skuse, who appeared for the detective, said Mr Pelletier's reaction to his client's joke was 'bizarre in the extreme.' Barrack-room jokes of this kind were 'not uncommon' in the police force, he explained. An example was that one policeman might be locked in a room by his colleagues with a stick of dynamite which they had lit, a statement which prompted the magistrate, Mr Jack Towers, to 'hope this sort of thing didn't happen in the Northern Territory police force.'

In a reserved decision, Mr Towers, dismissed a charge of aggravated assault against Detective Marchant, but found that the prosecution had proved a charge of common assault.

He said the incident at the Chopsticks had been a joke in 'appallingly bad taste.' The detective had been more inebriated than he had admitted on the night of the offence. But it was an undisputed fact that he had chased Mr Pelletier with a meat cleaver, that the solicitor had been 'extremely scared and had become hysterical,' and that the detective could not have known the effects on the solicitor would be as devastating as they were. 'I don't believe the defendant intended to harm Mr Pelletier [but] I believe Pelletier had rebuffed the defendant and the defendant was a trifle annoyed and decided to frighten the daylights out of him.'

To a very relieved detective, the magistrate did not record a conviction against him.

# JUSTICE UNDER THE MANGO TREE

It was during the annual build-up to the wet season in August, 1977 that a Darwin magistrate, for the first time in legal history, flew out to an Aboriginal settlement to preside over a court of summary jurisdiction.

Accompanied by this writer, Mr Lawrence Kirkman, chief stipendiary magistrate, chartered a single-engine Cessna and travelled to Oenpelli in Arnhem Land. As the court convened, it was surrounded by a large crowd of inquisitive Aborigines, many of whom had never left the settlement all their lives.

'Silence,' shouted Constable Allan Keyes. 'The Oenpelli Court of Summary Jurisdiction is in session,' but his words could barely be heard above the wind, the *gun-mayorrk*, which swept down from the Arnhem Land escarpment. Curious eyes switched to Mr Kirkman, who bowed solemnly to the assembly and took his seat under the shade of a huge mango tree. It was, he told his audience, an historic occasion. For the first time, a court of law was sitting at Oenpelli.

Overhead, a formation of white cockatoos flew by, screeching at the absorbed gathering below and deliberately timing their arrival, it seemed, like jet aircraft in a fly-past. Unperturbed, Mr Kirkman explained the administration of the law. It was not right, he said, that people should be made to attend court as far away as Katherine. This would be the first of regular sittings, but how often the court would convene would rest solely with the people who lived in and around the settlement. He hoped that, despite the beauty of the country, magistrates would not have to come out very often. Mr Kirkman concluded by intimating that Aboriginal Justices of the Peace would sit with the magistrate, advising him, or her, on matters of local concern.

The court then got underway. The thirty-two defendants sitting in the background, stirred uneasily. Defence solicitor, Mr Dyson Hore-Lacey, at that time working for Aboriginal Legal Aid, and police prosecutor, Sergeant Jack Nichol, squared their shoulders and shuffled their papers.

'Ronald Dirdi,' called Constable Keyes. Ronald detached himself sheepishly from the group, hesitated and walked forward. Mr Kirkman read the charge – taking liquor onto the Arnhem Land Aboriginal Reserve. Ronald pleaded guilty and Sergeant Nichol, his Irish brogue battling the *gunmayorrk*, read the facts. Mr Hore-Lacey spoke in mitigation and Ronald was fined thirty dollars. 'That penalty,' Mr Kirkman told him, 'is far less than is customarily imposed on people who breach that particular law. I only do that because this is the first court.'

The cases continued – disorderly behaviour on a reserve, malicious damage, drive under the influence, larceny, drunk on a reserve and aggravated assault. 'There's hardly one case before the court today,' observed Mr Hore-Lacey, 'that isn't connected with alcohol.'

By *banangarra* or lunchtime, about half the cases had been dealt with. When the court resumed at 1.30 only three defendants had turned up. By two o'clock, a few more had trickled back – but it was obvious their interest had waned. At 3.30 the court adjourned and the remaining spectators, five or six Aboriginal women, gathered their children and disappeared. The *gunmayorrk* rallied for one last effort, as if trying to blow the intruders away, and then gave up. Silence and tranquillity descended on the settlement.

The historic day was over.

Lawrence Kirkman took over as chief magistrate following the resignation of David McCann shortly after Cyclone

Tracy. Despite his severe visage that sometimes overawed defendants who appeared before him ('Christ, I guess I'll be going inside for ten years' one defendant on a minor charge muttered when he spotted him) he was respected for his fairness, good sense and practical wisdom.

Nor did he bow to pressure as was evinced in the case of Tony Belo, an East Timorese arrested for maintaining radio contact with Fretilin guerrillas during the bloody Indonesian occupation in 1976. Federal police, egged on by the Federal government, were more than anxious to get a conviction after going to great lengths to capture him, being frustrated by the fact that Belo kept eluding them by moving his transmitter from place to place. After weeks of searching they finally caught up with him driving along Bagot Road in Darwin – three car loads of them converging on his vehicle – and hauled him before Lawrence Kirkman who, after listening to the evidence, threw out the multiple charges that the Crown had laid against him. Much to the obvious chagrin of the police, the court erupted in loud cheering when the magistrate announced his decision. The Federal Police, it was said, left with their tails between their legs.

Lawrence is remembered with much affection.

# Note

The story of Justice Under the Mango Tree first appeared in the *Australian* newspaper.

# OLD MAN ROCK AND A BUDDHIST LEGEND

When the RAAF began using Old Man Rock for target practice, there was, justifiably, an outcry from the Larrakeyah tribe, for the rock is not only part of their Dreamtime but one of their most important sacred sites. Called the Dariba Nunggalinya, Old Man Rock is located off the Casuarina Coastal Reserve and is believed to be the final resting place of the first Larrakeyah man. According to the Larrakeyah people, Nunggalinya is responsible for earthquakes, storms and cyclones, including, of course, Cyclone Tracy. Such events, they believe, do not occur simply because of natural forces; they are provoked by human actions or failures. The legend of Old Man Rock was recounted by Andrew Henda, who lived at Bagot Reserve in Darwin, during the hearing of the Interim Aboriginal Land Commission on the Larrakeyah and associated Aboriginals' claim for the rock. And Andrew didn't mince his words.

'Old Man Rock,' Andrew said, 'in the sea near Casuarina, he started off somewhere near Koolpinya and he started to travel and he up stops where he sits down now. They reckon he had two wives; one of them she had a baby and he muck around with the other and kill her. Hurt her inside; he had a very big prick. That's why he started to run away from there. Then his balls got heavy and he couldn't go any further. When he was travelling he dragged his prick, made a creek – the one out Koolpinya way, Black Jungle. When his balls got too heavy, he sat down [and] the tide came and went over him. He had to stay there and that's where Old Man Rock is. Now RAAF drop bomb, people go fishing, he's probably getting weak now.'

Andrew said that his father had told him the story and also told him, 'That rock part of the Larrakeyah dreaming.'

The RAAF ceased using it as a bombing target and Old Man Rock was declared a sacred site.

It is interesting to note that the most famous of all Aboriginal sacred sites, Uluru – earlier know as Ayers rock – is intertwined with a Buddhist legend which has it that the founder of Tibetan Buddhism, Padma Sambhara, is living inside a rock. According to ancient chronicles, Sambhara left Tibet almost two thousand years ago for a distant land where he planned to teach Buddhist law. The land was located in the middle of a sea and its inhabitants were black. Sambhara, regarded as immortal, is said to live among them still in a red or coffee-coloured rock that corresponds in location and description to Uluru. Sambhara's rock is also associated with rainbows, and according to Aboriginal legend the great water serpent Wanampi, who lives under Uluru, is able to rise into the air in the form of a rainbow. Sambhara, Buddhists believe, was a master of serpent power.

Dreaming paths of the Aboriginal people, with their associated sacred sites, span great distances across Australia. The late Noel Wallace, who was an Associate Member, Australian Institute of Aboriginal Studies and Honorary Associate in Anthropology, Victoria National Museum, after a lifetime of research, recorded some twenty-two major mythic lines passing near the point where the Northern Territory, South Australia and Western Australia meet.

The Dreaming of the Kangaroo Totem stretched east to near Oodnadatta, west to near Kalgoorlie and north to near Papunya – some one thousand, two hundred kilometres east to west and six hundred kilometres north to south. The dreaming of the Honey Ant Totem stretches from Papunya in the north to the coast near Yalata in the south, about eight hundred kilometres. The Honey Ant mythic line branches into Western Australia via Docker Creek, which produces another line more than a thousand kilometres in length. Another dreaming path, known to the Bunitj clan, is linked with legend as far away as Yirrkala on the Gove Peninsular in the east and the Daly River, six hundred and fifty kilometres as the crow flies to the west – literally the width of the Top End.

No major myth, it is believed, runs less than many hundreds of kilometres and each has within its length dozens of sacred sites, places where the Totemic Ancestor taught the Aboriginal people's law. These sacred sites have existed, in Aboriginal law, since the beginning of time.

# THE FUTURE JUDGE AND
# THE WEDDING PARTY

It takes a fair leap of the imagination when one sees them sitting on the Bench, portentous, stern of visage and bewigged and gowned, that judges were once young solicitors appearing before the beak in the lower courts of summary jurisdiction, sometimes in distant places.

Geoff Eames, who became a Supreme Court judge in Victoria, once practiced in Darwin, appearing for defendants on minor charges like assault, hindering police or using indecent language. One case in particular comes to mind in which the future judge appeared, and it all began at the Tomlins' wedding party in Darwin.

All the immediate family was there and, of course, numerous relatives and friends. Young Chris Tomlins had been busy all day, preparing food, organising chairs and getting the drinks ready. Mother, Maria, and father, Ambrose, had also been hard at work to ensure its success. And, as it turned out, everyone was having a jovial old time... until an unexpected and uninvited guest in the portly shape of Detective Constable Barry Frew arrived.

From then on, to use the phraseology of Geoff Eames, 'a nightmarish experience began to transpire.' The 'cuddly' Frew (as a female admirer once called him) was there for two reasons. He had been told, mistakenly, that it wasn't a wedding reception at all, but a drug party. And he also wanted to talk to Chris about some unpaid fines and a breach of bond conditions. As three police officers waited nearby, Constable Frew showed Maria his search warrant. Maria told him, bluntly, that she didn't want her house searched. He then spoke to Chris, who, 'not being co-operative,' was promptly arrested.

What happened then was somewhat confusing, but in the words of the prosecutor, Graham Houston, 'several others intervened and tried to prevent Tomlins from being taken away.' Tony Tomlins, seeing what was happening to his brother, struggled with Frew. Maria also tackled Frew who lost control of Tomlins. Father Ambrose entered the fray, tackling Frew. Others joined in. A woman named Kay grappled with Frew while another police officer, hastily summonsed, grabbed Kay and they all spilled out into the road.

The upshot of it all was that Chris and his group were charged with hindering police. They changed their pleas to guilty after charges of assaulting police and escaping lawful custody were withdrawn. Said Geoff Eames, who appeared for Maria, Tony and Kay, 'It was an evening which had its own unique qualities. The events that occurred arose by someone telling police that a drug party was to be held at the Tomlins' house. What happened flowed from that malicious information. Of course, it wasn't a drug party. Up to when police arrived it was a very happy and pleasant event. It then collapsed into a chaotic and somewhat depressing series of events.' Mr Eames said a person of no less standing than the Attorney-General himself, Paul Everingham, had expressed his 'condolences' (perhaps mistaking it for a funeral) to the family for what had happened. Even the police had acknowledged that their actions had been precipitous. 'It was an event that no-one wants to look back on with too great a scrutiny,' he declared.

Solicitor David Parsons, who became a senior counsel at the Melbourne Bar and who appeared for Chris, said there had been 'an enormous amount of people all yelling and screaming.' And his fellow solicitor, Greg Borchers, who appeared for father Ambrose, said the sight of his wife being arrested was 'just too much for him.' Without proceeding to conviction, the magistrate discharged Maria and Kay, fined Tony and Michael Tomlins seventy-five dollars and Chris one hundred dollars. Ambrose, who, he accepted, had been clearly upset, got away with a twenty-five dollar fine. It had all been very disturbing for those present, the beak agreed.

# RUBY'S SWAN SONG

Ruby Willis was one of the stolen generation and her name was a by-word in Darwin. Her impromptu song and dance performances in the city's Tamarind Park during the 1970s entertained many a passer-by while her courtroom appearances invariably attracted an appreciative audience. She singled out well-dressed tourists and would harangue them mercilessly. When one buxom American tourist tried to ignore her, Ruby lifted up her T-shirt and said, 'You think you've got big ones; well, look at these.' On the other hand a generous visitor who offered a cigarette or two would be treated to a classic song in a surprisingly good voice.

She was particularly intrigued with a turban that a Darwin solicitor, Mr Sergit Sekhon, wore. Whenever she spotted Mr Sekhon she would call out, 'Hey there, wait' and attempt to grab the turban. Often the hapless Mr Sekhon could be seen running down the main street, Ruby in hot pursuit.

But behind Ruby's carefree exterior was a life dogged by tragedy. She lost lovers and children in tragic circumstances. In November, 1963, at Pine Creek Ruby was stabbed and a male friend murdered. As a young woman she lost a baby while swimming across the Adelaide River. The child had been ill for some time and Ruby had decided to walk to Darwin to seek medical aid. Her son, Brian, an Aboriginal Legal Aid Service director, died in Alice Springs at a young age.

Ruby Willis was born at Barrow Creek on December 26, 1932. In keeping with Government policy of the times, part Aboriginal Ruby was taken away from her mother and sent to the Methodist Mission at Croker Island, together with other children from various parts of the Territory. She was among a group of ninety-five mission children evacuated in 1942 after the island became the target of Japanese aerial attacks. The youngsters were transferred to Oenpelli. Then began an epic six-weeks, four thousand, eight hundred kilometre journey down the track to Adelaide, Melbourne, across to New South Wales and, finally, to a Methodist camp at Otford, south of Sydney. The exiles returned to Croker Island in 1946, sailing up the east coast on the *MV Reynella* and then across to their island in a smaller vessel. After leaving the mission school, many of the children, including Ruby, came to Darwin in search of work and a future. Ruby, then a fine looking young woman, met a crocodile shooter and went bush with him. Tough and resourceful, she quickly learned the tricks of the crocodile industry and one of the skills she picked up was taxidermy. She would stuff crocodile skins for sale, using marbles, collected by children, for the eyes.

As she grew older, Ruby began to appear regularly in the Magistrate's Court and was frequently jailed. But Ruby was never defeated by her court appearances, usually turning them into further opportunities for theatre. There were few members of the police force or magistrates who would not remember facing Ruby's indignant tirades. Former Chief Magistrate, Mr Gerard Galvin, said that Ruby was always 'good' with him, but other colleagues were not so lucky. He remembered one day dealing with a bunch or prisoners from the Darwin lock-up. Ruby was among them. 'She was leaving the court room and coming back, making a lot of noise each time. I told the police to keep her outside – resulting in a tremendous commotion. So Ruby appeared before me on a charge of disorderly conduct in the courthouse. When I asked her what she was doing in court that morning she couldn't tell me – apparently she had been put in protective custody for the night, released next morning, but simply tagged along to court with the rest of the prisoners still in custody.'

Fiercely independent, Ruby always refused help from Aboriginal Legal Aid officers and would not accept social security payments, despite the urgings of welfare officers. Ruby's last appearance in the Darwin Magistrate's Court before she was taken to Adelaide Hospital with a terminal illness was one of her best. Perhaps she sensed, somehow, it would be her swan song. A crowded gallery listened as the police prosecutor, Sergeant Kevin Maley, cleared his throat and began: 'Ruby Willis, you stand charged with behaving in a disorderly manner in Smith Street on July 10. How do you plead?'

'I didn't do that, mate,' replied Ruby, hitching up her frock.

'Ruby,' continued the sergeant, 'you also stand charged with behaving in a disorderly manner in the Commonwealth Bank. How do you plead?'

'Not me, mate, I was in Fannie Bay.'

And so the charges were read – resisting arrest, assaulting police and using objectionable language. Ruby spurned the services of Legal Aid, pleaded not guilty to all counts and said she would conduct her own defence.

Sandra Tregoning, a company director, told how Ruby called her a 'fucking moll' – not once but several times outside Woolworths.

Ruby (indignantly): 'I don't even know you, mate. I don't know you from a bar of soap.'

Sandra: 'She was swinging her arms and said to me: 'Who do you think you are, ignoring me?' She was obviously drunk.

'Hey, crumbs,' interrupted Ruby, 'I don't even know you.'

Magistrate Galvin, after vainly requesting Ruby to be quiet, ordered her to be removed from the court.

'Don't you manhandle me, you bastards,' warned Ruby, as two policemen descended on her. 'I'm staying here.'

As Ruby was hustled out, Sandra resumed her story and said she had been 'totally embarrassed.'

The next witness was Detective Constable Martin McPherson, but before he took the oath, Mr Galvin told a policeman to tell Ruby that if she behaved herself she could come back.

'I was in the Commonwealth Bank on July 10,' began the constable as Ruby reappeared and sat down.

'Ruby came in, in an agitated state and I heard her say, 'And fuck you too, mate.' She was standing next to me and I asked the bank officer to phone the police station. 'Which bank, mate?' asked Ruby, pre-empting the now well-known catch-line.

Constable McPherson, 'The Commonwealth.'

Ruby: 'I don't bank there.'

Constable Lorraine Kahlin then entered the witness box and said she and Constable Garner approached Ruby in the Smith Street Mall and told her they had received reports that she'd been shouting and swearing.

Ruby: 'God, it must have been my ghost.'

Constable Kahlin (continuing): 'She sat down on the footpath and refused to come with us.

Ruby: 'I'm not a grizzly bear.'

'She punched Constable Garner and me several times as we tried to get her off the ground.'

Ruby: 'What, me? Crumbs!'

'She continued to swear and struggle and we had to physically carry her 50 metres to the police van.'

Ruby, 'Not me, I've got legs.

'At the watch-house she continued to be aggressive.'

Ruby: 'She's telling a pack of lies.'

Magistrate Galvin, 'Ruby, that's enough.'

Constable Garner corroborated his colleague's evidence after being told by Ruby not to stutter.

Mr Galvin: 'Anything you want to ask him, Ruby?

Ruby: 'Yes. Hey, mate. I didn't speak to you. My golly, I was well and truly away.'

Prosecutor Maley: 'That's the case for the prosecution.'

Mr Galvin: 'Are you going to give evidence, Ruby?'

Ruby: 'Can't be bothered.'

Sergeant Maley began reading out Ruby's list of prior convictions, but was interrupted by the magistrate, 'That's enough for my purposes,' he said. 'Now Ruby, I want you to listen to me and I don't want you to stack on a turn. Is there anything you want to say?'

Ruby: 'Can't be bothered.'

Mr Galvin: 'Where have you been living lately?'

'Up on the hill.'

'Well, Ruby, you'll be going to jail for two-and-a-half months.'

Ruby's reply was inaudible. The court adjourned. The spectators left. The prosecutor mopped his brow with a handkerchief.

Only Ruby's voice could be heard, echoing along the corridor: 'Don't you manhandle me, you bastard.'

Ruby was only fifty-three when she died.

# REFLECTIONS ON TRACY

## THE TIME THE GREEN ANTS DISAPPEARED

There was an observation after Tracy that although the cyclone swept Darwin into the sea (well, some of it, anyway) it put the city on the map. There was a certain amount of truth in this because nothing much had happened there since the town was bombed by the Japanese thirty-two years previously – at least nothing much that attracted the interest of southerners apart from a fleeting moment of 'Cold War glory' in 1954 when Evdokia Petrov, the wife of defecting Russian spy, Vladimir Petrov, was rescued by Territory police when the aircraft on which she was being forcibly held by two KGB agents who had arrived in Australia to escort her back to the Soviet Union, landed in Darwin for refuelling. Although five recorded cyclones previously had devastated Darwin, it was only after Tracy that the city changed significantly. Until the advent of white settlers, the only record of a cyclone would have been a descriptive new song in the repertoire of the local Aboriginal tribe, the Larrakeyah.

In the first month after Tracy, Darwin was likened to 'an ant's nest disturbed,' its citizens 'rushing about fixing what they could without pause for reflection.' Incidentally, it was believed that Aborigines living in Darwin were forewarned of the disaster and quit the city because they noticed that all the green ants, prolific in the region, had disappeared. However, with a large influx of men and women from the south, the city became more sophisticated. After nearly a hundred years, it lost a lot of its old hell-raising image. No more did crocodile shooters release their crocs in public bars 'just for a bit of a laugh.' It was no longer an isolated outpost populated by a laid-back, casual community.

With the almost complete rebuilding of the city, the way of life altered, although initially, an ugly side reared its head with the erection of roughly painted signs along streets warning 'Trespassers will be shot. Keep out.'

The construction of new houses resulted in a carpet sales boom. Rarely purchased before the big blow, they became the biggest selling item, apart from beer, in the city. The local *NT News* was full of advertisements for carpets and carpet sales and just about every carpet company in the country sent their representatives to Darwin. Auctions were also held for Persian carpets, unheard of until then. Attitudes towards Aborigines also began changing including a far more guarded response by police to matters concerning them.

Part Aborigines, previously treated as scum by the police, began getting more vocal about land rights and their general rights before the law. The year before Cyclone Tracy, the Aboriginal Legal Aid Service was set up in Darwin and for the first time Aborigines began to get expert legal advice. There was also an influx of solicitors, chasing big money and mining companies began establishing public relations offices to justify their positions and their abuse of Aboriginal land. The granting of exploration licences was speeded up. In 1974, the year of the cyclone, not one exploration licence was granted. As the Mayor, Harold 'Tiger' Brennan lamented: 'If you go in and apply for a licence, you put your money in, it may be twelve months to two years. I have had an application in for four years. No one can go and work on it so you apply and wait and there is no work going on at all.'

Tracy's erratic fury also blew up business for escort girls. Agencies began appearing in Darwin. Thriving first on the custom of workers who poured in to help rebuild the city, the agencies struck a bonanza when highly paid miners employed at the uranium sites of Jabiru and Nabarlek began calling on their services. Apart from a few incidents including one in which a one-legged customer punched his escort in the face, breaking her upper denture because she complained about the position she had been forced to assume, the agencies managed to avoid publicity. Until, that is, the entire journalistic staff of Darwin's weekly newspaper resigned over the refusal of a company executive to publish a story on allegations by an Adelaide-based agency, Patties, that its recently opened business was being singled out for police harassment. Head of Darwin CIB, Chief Inspector John Maley, confirmed that as a result of raids two people had been charged under the seventy-five-year-old Suppression of Brothels Act. But when Crown solicitors finally unearthed the Act they found the maximum penalty for a first offence had not been amended since the days of Edward VII. It remained at twenty pounds.

Fifteen months after the event the Darwin Disaster Welfare Council issued its final report. Copies – and only a few were printed – have all but disappeared. Prominent people were asked to relate their 'personal response' to Tracy and among them was the argumentative Jim Bowditch, (mentioned in a previous chapter) long-term Darwin commentator, Walkley award winner and until 1973 editor of Darwin's daily newspaper.

> I was pretty sloshed when Tracy began moving in on Darwin because with some thousands of other people I was celebrating a normal Darwin Christmas eve party which are pretty boozy. At the party I had listened to the warnings about Tracy approaching and like most other people I ignored them as we had often had warnings of this nature over the years and nothing had happened. Next I remember being woken by my wife about midnight, and still didn't believe that anything was happening and feeling pretty ill. However, it did come clear but I am not sure that the drama of our house is of much interest

to you, but it did blow apart and I did in fact get trapped between the floor and the ceiling and walls when I whipped upstairs to try and rescue the cat. After a couple of hippies from over the road had helped me out from the wreckage next morning we decided to go and see what happened to the town.

With no water to drink, no transport, no dry place to sleep, no power available, and people 'digging holes all over the place and going to the toilet out in the open at Casuarina High School' the authorities decided that ten thousand people should be evacuated. And here Bowditch made a pertinent point.

I do think it was a mistake to rush the women out; I go along with the view that far too many men were left here and quite useless and contributed nothing; there isn't any doubt at all that the general morale of the place would have remained higher. From my observations I think that the women reacted and behaved in a much better manner than a majority of men. The reaction of a very large number of blokes was simply to get hold of a bottle and get sloshed and stay that way for days and days. I would say that a very large percentage of the men who stayed behind were under the influence of liquor despite the attempts by Stretton (Major General Alan Stretton who exercised supreme control over Darwin's forty-five thousand residents for six days after Tracy) to stop the sales of booze. The fact of the matter was that there were vast quantities of it stolen and there were still any number of outlets in town selling liquor including hard stuff right from the beginning despite Stretton's order that there was to be none.

Bowditch claimed (and if this was true it was kept well under wraps) that Ray McHenry, first assistant secretary to the

Department of the Northern Territory, who was appointed to co-ordinate 'all the things that were being done' and was tagged by the local press as Supremo, had been working on a disaster plan for months prior to Tracy and had set up committees in Katherine and Alice Springs. But he wasn't planning for cyclones, but for war. Bowditch could well be correct, as McHenry did at times confide in the journalist. It was because of McHenry's prior planning that the evacuation 'and the looking after people' worked so well. It was, says Bowditch 'as good as possibly could have been expected.'

Bowditch gives a not very flattering account of Darwinians.

> I have always believed,' he wrote, 'that the Darwin community was a spoilt community, had an absolute ball in a pretty good climate, pretty well paid for very little work, fares out every two years, getting all sorts of concessions out of the government on the claim that living in the tropics is harder. But the Public Service Board and Government has been conned for years if this were the situation. I think that as a result of being a spoilt community many people did crack up during the hard times because we were soft: I don't go along with the rugged Territory image that some people try to protect. There are certainly plenty of rugged Territorians but they do not live in Darwin but out in the scrub and stations and, mines and doing it hard, those are the sort of Territorians I think of deserving of the rugged image. Darwin people are mainly city people who come here from any one of the capital cities, move into this very comfortable situation and when it got blown away I frankly don't think they coped any better than most soft people would cope in such a situation.

[After the initial reaction to the cyclone, when the population] acted more like human beings [and] were more considerate and kinder to others because all were in the same boat, [the scene changed and people] drifted back to the old way of every man for himself and do his own thing. And now I think it is a petty city of heavy rip offs on the commercial front and the family units here are just trying to get together as much brass as they can, many I am sure with the object of getting out.

In his book *The Furious Days* Major General Stretton expressed a somewhat different view.

Words cannot describe the courage of the tattered residents of Darwin who, having lost every thing, came out of the ruins of a capital city and stoically set about bringing order out of chaos. In some miraculous way, as has happened previously in our history, a group of Australian had turned tragedy into triumph.

Like many others, my wife and I lost almost everything in Tracy. For the first day my wife had only her see-through nightie to wear, but no one took any notice. Looking back to that Christmas and the events that followed I wonder who is right – Bowditch or Stretton. And my conclusion is that both are.

## Sources

Major General Alan Stretton, *The Furious Days: The Relief of Darwin*, Sun Books, Melbourne, 1976